FRASER
ISLAND
AND COOLOOLA

The Author

John Sinclair has led the compaign to protect Fraser Island since 1971, when he formed the Fraser Island Defenders Organisation. He is also active in many other conservation organisations.

Born and bred in Maryborough, John Sinclair inherited a love of Fraser Island from his family. He has explored the region on foot, by boat, by air and in off-road vehicles. His research for the many forums in which he has advocated the conservation of Fraser Island, and his participation with leading scientists in exploring the wonders of both Fraser Island and Cooloola, have made him an authority on the area. His campaign to protect the island has resulted in a number of court battles, including a successful case in the High Court which resulted in 'public interest' being defined in Australia. In 1977 he was named as Australian of the Year by the *Australian* newspaper for his part in the compaign to protect Fraser Island from sandmining.

John Sinclair has written a number of books on the Great Sandy Region and has been a leading figure in the movement to have the region placed on the World Heritage List. He has had a longstanding interest in Australia's national parks and natural areas. He now lives in Sydney.

Additional photography in this book is by:
Gunther Deichmann
Leo Meier
Neil Morrison
Scott Needham
Stephen Nutt

Front cover:
Lake MacKenzie is one of the unique perched dune lakes of the Great Sandy Region.

Endpapers:
Rippled sand in the Great Sandy Strait.

Previous page:
Hibiscus etches the shores of Lake Cootharaba.

Right:
Defying gravity, Fraser Island's mobile sand is swept forward to engulf the forests in its path.

Back Cover:
The giant satinay is a majestic and dominant rainforest tree on Fraser Island.

FRASER ISLAND
AND COOLOOLA

JOHN SINCLAIR
PHOTOGRAPHY BY REG MORRISON

Black-headed pardalote (*Pardalotus striatus*).

Published by Lansdowne Publishing Pty Ltd
Level 5, 70 George Street, Sydney NSW Australia 2000

First published by Weldon Publishing 1990
Reprinted by Ure Smith Press 1991
Reprinted (limp edition) by Lansdowne Publishing Pty Ltd 1995

© Copyright: Lansdowne Publishing Pty Ltd 1990
© Copyright design: Lansdowne Publishing Pty Ltd 1990

Editor: Sheena Coupe
Designer: John Bull, The Book Design Co.
Assembly: Michelle Havenstein
Map: Stan Lamond

Typeset in 12½ point Bembo by Savage Type Pty Ltd, Brisbane
Produced in Hong Kong by Mandarin Offset

National Library of Australia Cataloguing-in-Publication data

Sinclair, John, 1939–   .
Fraser Island and Cooloola.

Bibliography.
Includes index.
ISBN 1 86302 476 X.

1. Fraser Island (Qld.) — Description and travel.
2. Cooloola National Park (Qld.). 3. Fraser Island
(Qld.) — Description and travel — Views. 4. Cooloola
National Park (Qld.) — Pictorial works. I. Title.

994.32

Pages 4–5: Sunrise on Waddy Point, the most easterly
point of the Great Sandy Region.

Pages 6–7: Lakeside paperbarks and grass trees in the
Cootharaba landscape.

Right: Ancient coloured sands are exposed by erosion.

CONTENTS

MAP 13

THE GREAT SANDY REGION 15

THE LOST GENERATIONS 45

EXPLORERS AND SETTLERS 73

THE COASTAL SANDMASS 97

CLOTHING THE SAND 129

A LAND OF LAKES 169

FISH, FOWL AND OTHER FAUNA 197

FIGHTING TO THE FUTURE 219

FURTHER READING 250

ENDNOTES 252

ACKNOWLEDGEMENTS 253

INDEX 254

Above

*M*orning mists rise from Lake Cootharaba at Elanda Point.

Left

*W*anggoolba Creek meanders under a dense rainforest canopy.

A remnant of an ancient tree engulfed by sand
has been exhumed, undermined and sand-blasted
by the wind.

Now that so many small groups are emerging to
defend their own particular loved areas — their
dunes and reefs and remaining bits of bush and trees
— we need to be able to unite and widen that
devotion and give it a broader aim and meaning.
We are beginning to see that 'nature' and 'man' are
not separate, that each needs the other.

Judith Wright

N
BUNDABERG
HERVEY BAY
SANDY CAPE
ROONEY POINT
MARLOO BAY
Wathumba Swamp
Orchid Beach
WADDY POINT
INDIAN HEAD
PLATYPUS BAY
GREAT SANDY NATIONAL PARK
L Bowarrady
FRASER ISLAND
Cathedral Beach
HERVEY BAY
WOODY ISLAND NATIONAL PARK
Happy Valley
CORAL SEA
GREAT SANDY STRAIT
L McKenzie
Central Station
L Birrabeen
Ungowa
Eurong
FIVE MILE BEACH
MARYBOROUGH
L Boomanjin
SEVENTY
Dilli Village
Mary R
INSKIP POINT
HOOK POINT
WIDE BAY
Tin Can Bay
Rainbow Beach
DOUBLE ISLAND POINT
SOUTH
PACIFIC
OCEAN
COOLOOLA NATIONAL PARK
Noosa R
Mary R
GYMPIE
L Cooloola
L Gootharaba
Boreen Point
L Cooroibah
LAGUNA BAY
Tewantin
Noosa Heads
0 5 10 15 20 25 30
kilometres
FRASER ISLAND
AND
COOLOOLA

THE GREAT SANDY REGION

Wind has been both the creator and the sculptor of the Great Sandy Region by amassing and shaping vast volumes of sand. Almost every attribute of Fraser Island and Cooloola, in southern Queensland, is a product of the persistency and power of the winds that have carried the sand there, swept it up into a huge mass and then brought the rain to nourish the region's lush vegetation.

For countless thousands of years, the rivers of eastern Australia have eroded the land east of the Great Dividing Range, bleeding their lodes of alluvium downstream and eventually pouring them into the Pacific Ocean. The prevailing south-easterly winds have then swept this sand north in the surf zone. The sand has accumulated during the ages at a number of points, mainly abutting rocky headlands, to form the great sandmasses of eastern Australia — Cooloola, the islands of Moreton Bay, and the greatest sandmass in the world, Fraser Island. Over more eons, these sandmasses were colonised by a rich diversity of plant communities. The interaction of the wind with the sand and vegetation has worked and reworked the sand into an incredible wind-sculptured wilderness.

The process of sculpting the world's greatest sandmass began more than 400 000 years ago. The wind has shaped the coastline by its strength and direction; it has created and modified the rugged contours of its surface; it has brought the nutrient aerosols, collected by sweeping across thousands of

Above

The sun sets over Hook Point at the convergence of Fraser Island, Cooloola, Tin Can Bay and Great Sandy Strait.

Left

Lake Wabby was formed by a sandblow damming up a creek.

Facing page
Sandblows are one of the
more remarkable features of the
dynamic landscape of the
Great Sandy Region.

kilometres of the Pacific Ocean, to fertilise the ostensibly barren sand; it carries the rains to nourish the aggressive vegetation. The wind then determines which plants can grow by submitting them to its salty blasts. The wind is responsible for the rain that begins the processes between Sydney and Brisbane, hundreds of kilometres to the south.

Weathering erodes the ageless rocks of the New England region and fractions of this parent rock have been washed into countless streams. As this coarse gritty material is swept down the streams, it is tumbled and tossed, rolled and rattled to a state of refinement. In the sea, many grains of fine sand remain suspended in the turbulent waters of the wind-tossed surf where further agitation occurs as the grains roll along the ocean pipeline. The prevalent wind along Australia's east coast causes the waves to break mainly from the south. This drives the sand in suspension in the surf along the spiral which swivels it northward through the pipeline. The sand is further refined as it is slowly conveyed to its final resting place in the Great Sandy Region.

In the journey to the north, some of the sand becomes trapped on the southern side of bars and headlands that create congestion in the flow. Some sand is also diverted to lesser sandmasses, such as the frontal dunes along the north coast of New South Wales, the Gold Coast or the Moreton Bay islands.

The wind loses some of its impetus as it reaches the lower latitudes of Queensland, and the waves become less violent. Without such velocity, the waves leave some of their load of sand on the beaches. From the beaches, the freshly deposited sand is swept on to the vine-embroidered foredunes where it is trapped. Fraser Island and Cooloola's eastern beaches have been the principal beneficiaries of the ocean-borne sand.

Having created a dynamic foredune, which is gradually increasing in size in much the same way as a snowball, the wind plays a further role as it exploits any weaknesses of the dune and begins to carve into it. The dislodged sand aggravates the instability of any unconsolidated sand on the surface and so the wind begins sweeping sand forward. In the process, the wind buries forests lying in the path of the blown sand, suffocating the living forest under metres of sand. Eventually, after many centuries, it will exhume the skeletons of those same forests. While some sand is being reworked into an incredibly rugged terrain, the wind is performing yet another trick. It is carrying both rain and aerosols to nurture the luxuriant vegetation.

There are limits to the benefits of wind and rain, as the older dunes can attest. Eventually, rain leaches the nutrients from the topsoil deeper into the subsoil until most plant nutrients are out of reach of even the deepest roots. The plant communities become more stunted as the topsoil is increasingly impoverished. The rain also has another consequence. The raindrop splash effect wears away the steep slopes of the older dunes and causes more grains of sand to move down the slope. In this process the topography of the dunes becomes progressively more subdued.

The creative force of the wind is apparent everywhere one looks in this wind-shaped wilderness. Almost every tree surrenders to the force of the prevailing wind, leaning with it. On exposed areas plants are sculptured and tossed to become almost prostrate. Some of the trees are hedged by the wind. Most tree trunks have significantly more lichens, mosses, orchids or other epiphytes on the southern side, which receive more moisture. The wind even determines which plants will grow in what areas. Plant communities are arranged in a series of bands, ranging from those such as the pandanus and beach oaks which grow only in the most exposed areas to those that require the protection of the closed vine forests.

From the description of the power of the wind, it might be assumed that the Great Sandy Region is constantly lashed by strong gales. This could not be further from the truth. Even quite gentle breezes of 12 kilometres per hour are sufficient to sweep the surface of wet sand. However, most of the wind action occurred in past eras when different sea levels generated much stronger wind velocities. Now, the action of the wind is much less active, with only a very occasional cyclone reaching these latitudes.

LOCATION AND CLIMATE

The Fraser Island and Cooloola sandmasses form the core of the Great Sandy Region. The region also includes the scribbly gum dominated forest, or 'wallum', in the upper catchment of the Noosa River, the marine areas of Hervey Bay and Breaksea Spit, and the estuaries of the Great Sandy Strait and Tin Can Bay.

The region's southern point is located opposite Noosa Heads in south-east Queensland, approximately 120 kilometres north of Brisbane. On its eastern boundary, the region stretches approximately 185 kilometres north to

*T*he wind sweeps, and sandblows spill over to engulf the surrounding vegetation.

Sandy Cape at the tip of Fraser Island. Hervey Bay forms the north-western part of the region. To the west of the two sandmasses lie important natural estuarine areas. Great Sandy Strait lies between the southern part of Fraser Island and the coastal lowlands of the mainland. Adjacent to the northern end of Cooloola, Tin Can Bay is an estuary branching off the Great Sandy Strait providing a rich habitat for both fish and fowl. The very southern edge of the region is etched by the lakes of the Noosa River — Cooroibah, Cootharaba, Como and Cooloola. The region encompasses the entire catchment of the upper Noosa River upstream of Lake Cootharaba.

Hervey Bay, the very large embayment between Fraser Island and the mainland, was named by Captain Cook after John Augustus Hervey, who later became an admiral of the British navy. The name now also applies to the city that has grown up at the base of the bay. With a population of over 20 000, Hervey Bay is the main service centre of and access point to Fraser Island. The other principal service centre of the region is Rainbow Beach township. Other lesser service centres are Noosa Heads, from which day trips are organised to both Fraser Island and Cooloola, and Tin Can Bay, which mainly services the fishing fleets and recreational fishers using the Great Sandy Strait and the estuary. There are other small fishing villages at Boonooroo, Maaroom, Poona and Tinnanbar on the mainland side of the Great Sandy Strait and Teewah on the beach of the same name.

The Great Sandy Region has an area exceeding 500 000 hectares, consisting of five main components. With their approximate areas they are:

Fraser Island	184 000 hectares
Cooloola sandmass	28 000 hectares
Wallum in the catchment of the Noosa River	20 000 hectares
Hervey Bay and Breaksea Spit marine areas	300 000 hectares
Great Sandy Strait and Tin Can Bay estuaries	40 000 hectares

The region experiences a subtropical maritime climate with generally moderate temperatures, although the varied topography and vegetation result in quite a deal of microclimatic variation. For example, frosts, virtually unknown on the coast, may occur in the interior of Fraser Island.

Climatic records have been kept for over a century at the Sandy Cape lighthouse on the northern tip of Fraser Island. Here, the mean temperatures recorded are maximum 28.6 degrees Celsius and minimum 20.7 degrees Celsius. Average rainfall for Sandy Cape is 1263 millimetres. The rainfall increases on the island's west coast at Ungowa to 1740 millimetres and in the highest dunes in the centre of the island reaches over 1800 millimetres. Records from the Double Island Point lighthouse show annual mean temperatures ranging from 26 degrees Celsius to 15 degrees Celsius. Rainfall there averages over 1370 millimetres per year.

*T*he major service centre for Fraser Island is the nearby mainland city of Hervey Bay.

Overleaf

*T*he poisonous cycad *Macrozamia* was a staple food of regional Aborigines who mastered the skill of removing its toxic properties.

FRASER ISLAND

Resting at the southern end of the Great Barrier Reef, Fraser Island has a number of links with the reef. The most southern cay of the Great Barrier Reef, Lady Elliot Island, lies only 80 kilometres north of Sandy Cape. However, Breaksea Spit, a submarine extension of Fraser Island, stretches for 35 kilometres of that distance. The Great Barrier Reef diffuses the energy of the waves hitting the mainland shore. This reduces the volume of sand carried in the littoral zone north of Fraser Island and prevents the formation of extensive sandmasses further north. Fraser Island sits along the edge of the continental shelf, protecting the adjacent mainland coast from the worst of the buffetings of the seas whipped up by cyclones and storms in the Coral Sea, and it forms a safe channel for small boating.

Fraser Island is a magnificent mosaic of plant communities, lakes, swamps, sandblows, beaches and wetlands. Its outstanding features include 20 kilometres of spectacular cliff faces of brilliant coloured sands, rugged volcanic outcrops, over forty dune lakes, extensive and colourful wildflower-strewn heathlands, tall dense rainforests, some towering above clear freshwater streams, and vast surfaces of mobile sand moving across the landscape.

The island stretches 123 kilometres from north to south with an average breadth of 14 kilometres, ranging up to 22 kilometres at its widest part. The dunes reach a height of 240 metres. Unlike the deserts, Fraser Island — the world's largest single sandmass — supports a diversity of vegetation. Huge volumes of fresh water add to the island's attraction. Water seeps from the dunes across the beach in innumerable soaks and fills picturesque creeks which flow through rainforest. Each of the lakes has an individual character and charm. Some are surrounded by heathlands, some by open forest, and others by rainforests. Some have startling white beaches. Some have water the colour of tea; others have crystal clear water to depths of 10 metres.

Despite being almost half the size of the Indonesian island of Bali, Fraser Island has a permanent resident population of only about 100 people, compared with Bali's population of over two million. The few permanent residents are mainly associated with tourism, the timber industry or the Sandy Cape lighthouse. However, a large mainland-based population works in the Fraser Island tourist industry. It is estimated that almost 500 000 visitors come to Fraser Island each year. There are three major tourist settlements: Orchid Beach in the north was built around a hotel established in 1968; Happy Valley, midway along the ocean beach, was established in the 1930s; Eurong, established in 1963, has grown rapidly to have the largest resident population. There are also some lesser settlements, a Forestry Department camp at Ungowa and two families staffing the lighthouse at Sandy Cape.

About two-thirds of Fraser Island is a state forest with about one-third making up the Great Sandy National Park at the northern end of the island. A small part of Fraser Island (less than 1000 hectares) is freehold land. The remainder, along the east coast, is vacant crown land.

*A*ttracting over 1000 visitors on many days, the banks of Wanggoolba Creek have now been protected by boardwalks.

*L*ake McKenzie, over 5 metres deep, covering more than 150 hectares
and sitting 100 metres above sea level, is one of the region's extraordinary
perched dune lakes.

*A*ncient coloured sands are among the region's greatest treasures.

Fraser Island is still largely an unspoilt wilderness. Scientists have declared that it is to the world's sandmasses what the Great Barrier Reef is to the world's coral reefs. The island is rich in both mineral sands and timber resources, and has been a major focus of conservation interest for almost a century. The conflict between conservation and exploitation brought Fraser Island to the centre of Australia's largest nature conservation controversy in the 1970s. Its significance was recognised in 1976, when it became the first item to be listed on the Register of the National Estate.

THE DUNES OF COOLOOLA

The soft sound of the breeze whispering in the cypress pines of the sand dunes crooned a low mournful wail, inspiring the Aboriginal name *Cooloola*. Now 'Cooloola' applies not only to the cypress pines that fringe the sandmasses; it has become the name for a region of elevated dune lakes and towering forests growing in deep sand. The enchanting scenery and majesty of the Cooloola sandmass is compressed into a long triangular area lying between Tin Can Bay, the Noosa River and the Pacific Ocean. The wallum catchment of the serpentine Noosa River is also included in the Cooloola National Park. Double Island Point, the lynchpin of the Cooloola sandmass, thrusts into the surging Pacific Ocean like a defiant clenched fist. It is a headland of almost 20 hectares of igneous rock, known to the Aborigines as *Gullirae*. It rises almost 95 metres out of the sea, and plays a strategic role in the development of the sandmass and the stability of the coastline.

Cooloola is only 150 kilometres north of Brisbane and can be reached within three hours in the comfort of the family car. Its proximity to Noosa, and its value as the closest coastal wilderness north of Brisbane, increase its appeal to those who want to escape from the superficiality of the concrete jungles and communes of industry. Cooloola's magic has encouraged many to work to preserve it, and has inspired others to paint, to write, to create. Judith Wright has written several poems inspired by Cooloola, including 'At Cooloolah' which concludes:

> White shores of sand, plumed reed and paperbark,
> clear heavenly levels frequented by crane and swan —
> I know that we are justified only by love,
> but oppressed by arrogant guilt, have room for none.
>
> And walking on clean sand among the prints
> of bird and animal, I am challenged by a driftwood spear
> thrust from the water; and, like my own grandfather,
> must quiet a heart accused by its own fear.

*T*he rich marine life is nourished by the many mangrove-lined streams
that feed into a well-protected Hervey Bay.

HERVEY BAY AND OTHER MARINE AREAS

Hervey Bay is enclosed between the mainland on the west and Fraser Island
on the east. The bay is very large, about 60 kilometres wide and 65 kilometres
from north to south. There is surf inside the bay only when strong northerly
winds blow across the exposed waters. The normally calm water makes
Hervey Bay a haven for small boating. Because of its sheltered location, the
bay was also favoured by the Australian fleet for its naval carrier manoeuvres.

More than 85 000 hectares of seagrass has been mapped in the bay, and
researchers believe that Hervey Bay has the most extensive seagrass beds in
eastern Australia, extending to a depth of 22 metres. The seagrass is an
important habitat for the marine mammal, the dugong (*Dugong dugon*). In
1988 the dugong population of Hervey Bay was estimated at between 1600
and 2300. Dugongs were heavily predated by European Australians who
boiled them down for oil in a factory at Bogimbah on Fraser Island until the
1940s. More recently, significant numbers have been drowned in shark nets
and others have been killed in trawl nets.

Turtles extensively use the waters of Hervey Bay. Although some
occasionally nest on Fraser Island beaches, they generally find the sand too
fine, preferring the coarser sand of mainland beaches on the western side of
Hervey Bay such as the Mon Repos rookery near Bundaberg. Mon Repos
has an international reputation as a major loggerhead rookery, and is also used
by green turtles and flatbacks.

*L*oggerhead turtles use Hervey Bay for courtship and mating.

*G*rey mangroves etch almost all the protected marine shores of the region.

*I*n early spring, hundreds of migrating humpback whales spend two
to five days in Hervey Bay.

Coral growth occurs in Hervey Bay at the head of the Great Sandy Strait surrounding Woody Island (*Tooliwah* to the Aborigines). There are many coral reefs close to its western shores. An artificial reef of more than 2500 car bodies, 800 tonnes of concrete rubble, 12 000 car tyres and four 20-metre steel barges (once used to remove Fraser Island timber) has been created just north of Woody Island. Since its beginnings in 1968, the reef has been remarkably successful in enhancing fish and marine life in the area.

Humpback whales (*Megaptera novaeangliae*) are among the most spectacular features of Hervey Bay's marine life. These giants of the sea were nearing extinction before exploitation ceased in 1963. They now breed in the waters of the southern Great Barrier Reef and appear in abundance in Hervey Bay from mid-August to mid-October. Over 200 whales have been counted in the bay, mainly around Platypus Bay near the Wathumba Creek estuary on Fraser Island. It appears to be a favourite area for mating, and for mothers and calves to rest before migrating back to Antarctic waters.

The Estuaries

Great Sandy Strait and its offshoot, Tin Can Bay, make up the fifth largest enclosed embayment on Queensland's coastline. At the northern end, the Great Sandy Strait is 10.5 kilometres wide; at its southern end at Inskip Point it is only one kilometre wide. Its channels are 15 to 25 metres deep.

The heavier sediments from the Mary River, which discharges into the strait, are swept north into Hervey Bay by strong tidal currents. Some larger

*R*ed mangroves, supported by prop roots, thrive in this sandy environment.

grained sediments accumulate south of Woody Island, which lies across the northern entrance of the strait. Finer riverine silts and muds drift from the Mary River south to the centre of the strait where the tide from the south meets the tide from the north. The meeting of the tides causes a large depositing of silt and the greatest accumulation of mud banks, islands and mangroves in the region. Stewart Island (*Coonangoor*), Dream Island, the Moon Boon Islands, a patchwork of mangrove islands and the huge wetlands complex of Boonlye Point are testimony to the accumulation of silt.

There are 16 300 hectares of mangrove in the Great Sandy Strait alone, and thirteen species have been identified. These trap silt, stabilise the shores, and through their prodigious leaf drop of almost 200 tonnes per hectare per annum, provide one of the most significant inputs into the marine food chain. A further 3700 hectares of saltmarsh lines the Great Sandy Strait, mainly on its western side between Boonooroo and the Mary River heads behind the pickets of mangroves that line the waterways. About 12 300 hectares of seagrass, of six different species, grows in the strait, most of it close to the centre. Seagrasses are extremely important in the estuarine food chain. They provide shelter for small and juvenile fish, prawns and other marine creatures, and valuable grazing for dugong.

Known to Aborigines as *Tindchin*, after a species of mangrove, Tin Can Bay now refers to both the estuary that branches off the Great Sandy Strait and the small township on its western shore. It is the base for about 250 commercial fishers working more than eighty trawlers. More than 70 000 kilograms of prawns, 10 000 mud crabs and 100 000 kilograms of fish pass through Tin Can Bay fish merchants annually.

Tin Can Bay and the Great Sandy Strait have one of the least disturbed watersheds of any Queensland estuary. The area has been remarkably stable with virtually no significant alteration to any bar or bank in fifty years. Much of Tin Can Bay and Great Sandy Strait is protected as Fisheries Habitat Reserves because the fish caught there have relied on estuarine areas during some stage of their development. To protect the fishing resources of amateur anglers not only in the estuaries, but also along the surfing beaches of Cooloola and Fraser Island, it is illegal to dig or fill or dump in the sea or disturb any of the vegetation in the Fisheries Habitat Reserves. Although these reserves should be as inviolable as national parks, they have been modified, reduced and impugned significantly by developments sanctioned by the Queensland government.

The Wallum Areas

Wallum was a term used by Aborigines to describe the banksia that grew on the sandy soils of the region. To the Aborigine, whose diet included no sugar and little other sweetness, the honey dripping from the ripe wallum (*Banksia aemula* and *B. serrata*) flowers in the early morning dew was a delicacy indeed.

For a long time Europeans despised the wallum and its low potential for agricultural productivity. They destroyed much of the natural wallum forest that stretched along the Queensland coast and replaced many of the

Facing page

*L*oose sand is swept by both wind and tide to establish ever-changing patterns.

*A*borigines knew this plant, *Banksia serrata*, as *wallum.* They sought it for the honey that drips from its ripe stamens. The name has now been extended to cover the whole coastal lowland region of southern Queensland where the banksia occurs.

native forests with exotic pine plantations. During the 1960s, CSIRO sponsored a survey of the ecosystems of all the coastal lowlands of south-east Queensland. Researcher J. E. Coaldrake classified the wallum lands into twenty different landscapes, four of which described the Cooloola area. The sandmass was one landscape unit (Cooloola); the Noosa plain a second unit (Noosa). The area surrounding the Noosa River lakes was a third landscape system (Cootharaba) and the upper Noosa River catchment was named Womalah. The Womalah landscape contains about one-sixth of the species of flowering plants and ferns of Cooloola, 100 of which are restricted to these sandstone soils. The grey kangaroo and much of Cooloola's mammalian fauna is also found mainly in this landscape.

Some of the biological features of the wallum not found on the sandmasses include two boronias, *Boronia keysii* (rediscovered in 1971, near Kin Kin Creek, after having been lost for fifty years) and *B. rivularis*. Fine stands of the handsome *Banksia spinulosa* are also found only in this landscape, ensuring that all six varieties of south Queensland banksias are represented in the Cooloola National Park. Scribbly gums (*Eucalyptus signata*) were once much more extensive in southern Queensland. Most of their wallum habitat elsewhere has been cleared but they survive on the deep sands of Fraser Island and Cooloola where the Womalah landscape is their last bastion on sandstone-derived soils.

Meandering through the heart of the Womalah landscape is the upper Noosa River, popularly known as the Little Noosa although it is a well-defined stream between 2 and 6 metres wide lined with deep sandy banks and fringed with thickets of shrubbery growing mainly on a narow levee bank flanking the stream. This bank, only a few centimetres above the surrounding countryside, prevents the proper drainage of the flat expansive plains up to a kilometre wide on either side of the river.

Although the waterlogged ground will not support any large trees, it does support a profusion of spectacular wildflowers. This landscape becomes a riot of colour in late winter and early spring and provides one of the most significant habitats for the shy ground parrot (*Pezoporus wallicus*), which, although endangered throughout most of its range, is not uncommon in this area. The riverside vegetation of the Noosa River is crowned by about 12 hectares of an unusual vine forest which is all the more interesting because it appears only a hundred metres from the treeless Noosa plain.

*W*ildflowers such as this tea tree (*Leptospermum* sp.) bloom in profusion throughout the year in the Great Sandy Region.

RECREATION IN THE GREAT SANDY REGION

The Great Sandy Region attracts over half a million visitors per annum, and the numbers are increasing rapidly. Although most visitors are accommodated in the comfort of motels in Hervey Bay, Rainbow Beach or Noosa Heads and visit the region only for a day excursion, an increasing number use off-road vehicles and are prepared to camp to be closer to the environment.

The region has long attracted surf fishers who today are assisted by the greater availability of four-wheel-drive vehicles. Amateur anglers fish the

*O*n most mornings the early morning mists hang like a heavy shroud
over the valleys and depressions of the Great Sandy Region.

gutters off the surf beaches seeking whiting, bream, flathead and trevally. Between July and October, those with stronger hunting instinct seek the pelagic tailor which annually migrate from the south. There have been some legendary reports of tailor catches and huge freezers are quickly filled when the tailor are biting. Unfortunately, the tailor fishers have a bad reputation for fouling the beach with fish skeletons and litter. Other fish caught from the beaches or the rocky headlands include mackerel and oyster fish or golden trevally. Those who are prepared to venture offshore have a much wider choice of fish, including reef fish, and inside Hervey Bay there are both reef and estuary fish to be caught.

As the use of motor vehicles is limited by recreation area managers, more and more people are rediscovering the adventure of bushwalking. The region can challenge both the novice and experienced bushwalker, with a maze of forestry tracks criss-crossing the sandmasses. Little special equipment is needed for bushwalking, although sturdy footwear to keep out sand and prevent blistered feet, long trousers to protect against scratches, a good map and water-bottles are desirable. Drinking water can be obtained from springs and soakages along the beaches, the lakes and streams. The best time for bushwalking is from May to August, when the weather is not too wet, not too hot, there are few insects and plenty of attractions.

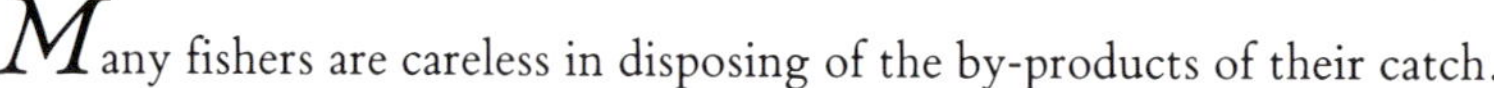

*M*any fishers are careless in disposing of the by-products of their catch.

*A*nglers compete for a place near Orchid Beach.

World Heritage Significance

The World Heritage significance of the Great Sandy Region was first recognised in 1974, just two years after Australia signed the World Heritage Convention. The other three areas then identified by the Australian Conservation Foundation, the Great Barrier Reef, South-West Tasmania and Kakadu, were listed in 1981.

In 1976, following the Fraser Island Environmental Inquiry, the Commonwealth government recognised the environmental significance of Fraser Island when it nominated it as the first item to be listed on the Register of the National Estate. Environment Minister Kevin Newman announced that he believed the Commonwealth government would give consideration to World Heritage listing for Fraser Island. The Queensland government has consistently opposed giving the area any international recognition, fearing that such recognition may inhibit its plans for future exploitation. In 1984, the Queensland government stated that it did not want 'one more inch of Queensland' included on the World Heritage List and refused to study the merits of the nomination of the Great Sandy Region. Because of this opposition, successive federal governments failed to assess the region's very significant World Heritage claims.

To qualify for World Heritage listing a nominated site must meet stringent standards of cultural or biological significance, physical or geomorphic dimensions or aesthetic quality. Sites may be listed on the basis of meeting just one criterion. For example, the Egyptian pyramids, Inca cities and many sites in the built environment are listed only under the criterion of cultural significance. In East Africa, the Serengetti National Park is listed on its biological significance. Mt Everest and the Grand Canyon are primarily listed on the basis of their physical credentials.

The Great Sandy Region deserves to be added to the World Heritage List not on the basis of just one of these, but on all four grounds. Culturally, archaeologists advise that Fraser Island is at least as significant as Lake Mungo in western New South Wales, which is already on the World Heritage List. Apart from archaeological relics, Fraser Island represents the complete tribal territory of at least one Aboriginal group in a relatively intact way. It also includes relics of post-European settlement.

The region has a threefold claim to outstanding biological significance based on the marine ecosystems of Hervey Bay, the Great Sandy Strait and Tin Can Bay, the terrestrial fauna, and the diverse mosaic of terrestrial flora. World Heritage listing would recognise the importance of Hervey Bay to whale migration, the significant dugong population, the marine flora, particularly in the littoral zone of mangroves and seagrass, and the rich and diverse biology of the tidal deltas of the Mary River in the Great Sandy Strait and in Tin Can Bay.

The region's fauna ranges from ground fauna, including earthworms and ants and other burrowing invertebrates which find sand a suitable medium in which to swim and crawl, to freshwater fauna such as fish,

*C*liffs of consolidated sand are one of the most remarkable features of the region.

*M*elaleucas line Lake Cootharaba at Boreen Point.

A giant satinay (*Syncarpia hillii*) draped in vines, stands firm and strong
in the Fraser Island rainforest.

amphibia, invertebrates and crustacea. Among the special birds are peregrine falcons and ospreys, white-breasted sea eagles, ground parrots and migratory waders, including curlews, godwits and whimbrels. The mammals include the purest strain of dingoes in eastern Australia and some native rodents.

The significance of the area's flora is the most obvious and outstanding biological claim for World Heritage listing. No sandmasses anywhere in the world have such grand forests. On Fraser Island and Cooloola, rainforests grow on dunes over 200 metres high. Among the largest trees are the satinays, which are virtually endemic to the region. The main element is diversity and the dramatic contrasts between plant communities growing in a dramatic mosaic in such close proximity. The region provides the best example in the world of retrogressive plant succession. As the soils become poorer the plant communities degenerate from rainforest to stunted heaths.

The most compelling reasons for World Heritage listing are the Great Sandy Region's geomorphological claims. Fraser Island is to sand dunes what Everest is to mountains; it is to sandmasses what the Great Barrier Reef is to coral reefs. The sheer bulk and size of the sandmass, and its great age and embodied history, excite awe and wonder. But the size is important only in that it enables the sandmass to contain the greatest representation of dune types found anywhere in the world.

The dynamic building and recontouring processes in the dunes are impressive demonstrations of a geomorphic process. They are as compelling in their awe as glaciers. The interaction of sand and vegetation is particularly significant, and the hydrology of the sandmass is extraordinary. Scientists have established that the mean residence time of water in the sand — that is, from the time it falls as a raindrop until it flows out to sea — is 100 years. Some of the water could have been percolating through the sand for over 200 years while some runs off almost instantly.

The lakes are very special. The region contains more than half the world's perched dune lakes. There are also numerous window lakes and barrage lakes such as Wabby Lakes where the streams have been dammed up by mobile sandblows. In an environment where it takes time to adjust to the notion of seeing lakes at all, the lakes are of exceptional scientific interest because of their freedom from major environmental impact.

The spectacular appeal of the lakes, coloured sands, rainforests, creeks, heathlands, expansive beaches and rugged rocky headlands makes the Great Sandy Region a place of special significance. Despite limited exploitation during the last 150 years, the area still retains its essential natural qualities. Extensive research has shown that the Great Sandy Region satisfies the stringent criteria adopted by UNESCO for inclusion in the World Heritage List. The first nomination elaborating on the region's claims was presented to both the Queensland and Commonwealth governments in August 1984. For more than five years the Queensland government has failed to address that nomination to assess its merits.

A melaleuca clings tenaciously to life as the wind reshapes the landscape near Lake Wabby. Some ancient melaleucas, the great survivors of sandblows, have withstood these forces for thousands of years.

THE LOST GENERATIONS

To the Aborigines, the Great Sandy Region was rich and productive. They lived on the rich fisheries along the coasts, in the estuaries and in the shallow lakes of the Noosa River. On the nearby Blackall Ranges they held bunya nut festivals. The abundance of fruit and game, the equable climate and glorious panoramic scenery provided for a productive and idyllic existence. It is small wonder that the Aborigines were fiercely possessive of their land and hostile to any intruders into their territory.

The region's human history is relatively short. Like a sleeping giant, the Great Sandy Region lay beside the savage Pacific Ocean for eons, assaulted only by the sea and the elements. The first human tenure of the region probably occurred early in the Aboriginal settlement of Australia, about 40 000 years ago. Through their rich oral history the Aborigines recorded events such as the interglacial periods when the sea levels were high and the times when the sea receded during the ice ages. They were healthy vigorous people whose culture was based on the sea and its harvest. Evidence of this is still found in the numerous middens of oyster shells and the shells of a bivalve mollusc which they called *ah-wong*.

The Aborigines of Fraser Island and Cooloola were generally well built and muscular. Their hair was usually jet black, and the men grew bushy curly whiskers and moustaches. They tied their hair in knots on the top of their head and used it as a receptacle for arrowheads and other personal possessions. Both sexes were extremely agile, and all went naked except for the pubic

Above
A stone scraper, exhumed by a sandblow near Lake Wabby.

Left
Wathumba Creek estuary is a notable fish nursery.

Caboonya, a Butchalla Aborigine, wearing a necklace of kangaroo teeth
and a seagull headdress.

aprons which they sometimes wore. For protection from the cold, rain or insects, fat from fish or animals, often mixed with ashes, was rubbed on the body. The main ornament was an elliptical piece of shell around the neck.

TRADITIONAL ABORIGINAL SOCIETY

Before the coming of Europeans four main Aboriginal groups dominated the Great Sandy Region. The Ngulungbara occupied the northern part of Fraser Island around Sandy Cape, and had no mainland territory. They claimed to be a separate tribe, but there are reports of intermarriage with Butchalla people to their immediate south. The Butchalla (or Batjala) occupied the central section of *Kgari* (Fraser Island; also reported as *Carree* and *Carina* in early records). The Butchalla also had a mainland territory which extended across the Great Sandy Strait to Bauple Mountain. They held all the land now covered by the settlements of Maryborough and Hervey Bay and the Tuan forestry plantation, as well as most of the islands in the Great Sandy Strait. The Dulingbara occupied the southern part of *Kgari*, and virtually all the Cooloola sandmass. Southern Cooloola and the area around Noosa was occupied by either the Kabi-Kabi or Chief Uwen Mundi's tribe.

The relationship between all these groups is not clear. According to F. J. Watson, who recorded *Vocabularies of Four Representative Tribes of South-East Queensland* just after the turn of the century, there were no major linguistic differences. His descriptions indicated that the whole region was occupied by the Kabi-Kabi people and that there were only minor dialect variances between the Aborigines of Fraser Island and those of the adjacent mainland. This leads to the speculation that all the Aboriginal groups, or hordes, were part of a grander Kabi nation which occupied the catchment of the Burrum, Mary, Noosa, Maroochy and Mooloolah rivers and all land between.

Both Matthew Flinders and James Cook commented on the numbers of Aborigines as they sailed past the Great Sandy Region. Ethnographer Dr Norman Tindale noted in 1974 that '[Fraser] Island would have been one of the more densely occupied areas of Australia, exceeded only by the Kaiadilt of Bentinck Island'. In a report tabled in the Queensland parliament in 1905, the State Protector of Aborigines, Archibald Meston, claimed that 'Fifty years ago, there were from 2,000 to 3,000 Aboriginals on Fraser Island, an exceptionally fine race of people. Today there are about twenty left on the island! . . . The food supply from the ocean and straits was unlimited. The big scrub supplied most of the vegetable diet . . . There were three dialects spoken . . . and the various tribes fought occasionally with each other and finished with a corroboree.'

Seasonally, Fraser Island was populated during the winter months when seafood was at its best. With the change of seasons, the summer territories on the mainland were reoccupied. Canoes made of a long single sheet of bark sealed at each end with beeswax were the major means of crossing the Great Sandy Strait. The canoes were used for fishing and hunting dugong and turtle, as well as for transport. Fire was carried in the canoes on a bed of sand or seaweed, and fish were cooked immediately they were caught.

*M*ill Point was known to Kabi Aborigines as *Wa-wa*, the place of crows.

*T*he large shield-shaped scar on this giant satinay near Central Station
was formed after Aborigines removed the bark in a single sheet to make
the roof of a gunyah.

For shelter, the Aborigines of the region cut strips of bark about 2.3 metres long into a shield shape and from them formed the roof of a semi-conical 'gunyah'. In winter this was warmed with possum skins and a fire at the entrance, and many suffered severe burns when they crawled too close to the fire on a cold night. The people moved as the seasons and food supplies dictated and on the death of a member of the group, but the gunyahs remained and may have been reused. Although they had no knowledge of agriculture, they used sticks to harvest a range of wild yams and other roots, particularly bungwall (*Blechnum* fern).

Many of the Europeans who mixed with the Aborigines in the early years of the twentieth century recorded their customs and traditions. Rollo Petrie, who went to live on Fraser Island in 1913, has provided much insight. He recalls one particular Aborigine named Nugget:

Nugget was a loner. He lived on the ocean beach in a little hut. He only visited the mainland from time to time, to spend the money earned from the teamsters. He would come back from the mainland looking sick and miserable. He would go off out to the beach to live on wongs and be fat and shiny the next time we saw him. Nugget would spend hours writing characters on sand and showing us kids where to get wongs at low tide and how to catch and cook fish. He also showed us how to catch yabbies in the creeks with sharpened sticks.

Petrie noted that the most remarkable feature of the Aborigines' fishing technique was the shortness of their fishing line. He said that Nugget's philosophy was to go to the fish and not wait for the fish to come to him.

Knives were made from stone, mainly a chert. Axes were of rock fastened to a wooden handle by gum and beeswax. All the rock for the tools and implements used on Fraser Island had to be imported. Most of it was probably quarried on Big Woody Island between Fraser Island and Urangan, but the rock of the axe heads appears to have come from much further afield. The Aborigines of Fraser Island had the same kind of weapons and implements as their mainland neighbours, except that they did not use woomerahs to project their spears further.

Bees featured largely in Aboriginal culture partly for their wax, which was used extensively, but mainly because their honey was a major source of sweetness. With a bland diet, the Aborigines craved what little sweetness they could obtain. Honey came either directly from the nests of the small native bees or from flowers such as banksias. The Aborigines licked the dew containing dissolved honey from the ends of the stamens of the ripe flowers and tracked the bees in flight to their nests after catching one and gumming a piece of fluff or feather to it. The significance of the bees to the culture cannot be underestimated; the proliferation of names like *Govi* and *Cubbih* creeks (names for a bee species) reflects the esteem in which they were held.

*S*tone cores such as this are still found on sites of Aboriginal tool making.

*A*borigines used this natural rock pool at Middle Rocks as an effective fish trap.

*S*tingless native bees, here gathering pollen from a guinea flower
(*Hibbertia* sp.), were valued for their honey.

*X*anthorrhoea or grass trees
provided a valuable food source.
Aborigines used the base of the
leaves as a type of cabbage.

The base of xanthorrhoea leaves was eaten either raw or cooked. In some seasons, Aborigines collected and roasted the fruit. Pandanus leaves were used to make baskets. The Aborigines also found a way of overcoming the poisonous properties of the fruits of the macrozamia. Before being mashed the ripe pineapple-like fruits were placed in dilly bags and soaked in running water for several days to leach out the toxic substances.

The Aboriginal social system was harsh and complex, with taboos and rituals of great importance to every member of the group. Polygamy was legal and widely practised. A man could not marry a woman of his own clan; children belonged to the clan of the mother. Cannibalism was practised, with the flesh of those killed in combat and those who died at an early age being eaten in a ritual act. No humans were deliberately killed to make a feast.

The bones of the deceased were dried and hung in a dilly bag in the hollow of a tree. Rollo Petrie described a burial tree at Central Station which he encountered as a child in about 1921:

The burial tree was a big Satinay with a hollow some 4–5 feet [1.5 metres] from the ground and extending some feet up the trunk. The tree was only a shell and probably 4–5 feet in diameter. They put the cleaned bones in a dilly bag. The dilly was hung on a forked stick, cut sufficiently long so as to keep the dilly clear of the ground when leaning against the wall. In this way many dillies could be placed in the same tree.

*P*andanus are common along the foredunes of Fraser Island and
Cooloola. Aboriginal women made baskets from their leaves.

To express sorrow in time of mourning, both men and women gashed themselves with sharp stones and other implements. The dead were highly respected and there is a record of a European being speared to death in the 1830s for taking a dilly bag from a burial tree.

Before the destruction of their tribal life, Aborigines were governed by a Council of Elders who determined punishments, conducted inquests, taught and explained the laws, customs and beliefs of their people. They also organised revenge expeditions. The Kabi were regarded as a fierce and hostile group. The men decorated their chests with cicatrices, ornamental scars of raised flesh, and some of the women amputated the first joint of the right-hand little finger, a practice common to mainland Aborigines of Moreton Bay. Every member of the tribe over six years old had the septum of the nose pierced, through which were worn pieces of bone or stick.

ESCAPED CONVICTS

The Aborigines were not the only victims of the establishment of the European settlement at Moreton Bay. Brisbane became a penal colony for long-term or difficult prisoners and the brutality, cruelty and inhumanity meted out to the convicts there drove many to escape. Some were prepared to risk their lives with the Aborigines, rather than succumb to the oppressive existence at Moreton Bay. Many perished, but a number were befriended by the Aborigines. They were integrated into tribal life and became 'white blackfellows' or *bunders*.

The *bunders* were accepted into Aboriginal society with surprising ease because of the Aboriginal belief in reincarnation. All the convicts who lived with the people and related their stories were claimed as reincarnations of deceased Aborigines. Their pale skin, altered appearance and lack of language were assumed to indicate the spirits of departed relatives. Widows sometimes claimed them as their former husbands.

Three notable escapees lived in Kabi territory: John Graham, David Bracefell and James Davis. They found themselves among kindred spirits, refugees from the aggressive expansion of an alien civilisation. John Graham, a diminutive Irishman, was convicted at age 24 to seven years transportation for stealing three kilograms of hemp. He escaped from Brisbane in 1827 and 'married' a widow, who died within a year. Graham remained with the people of the Cootharaba area for six years but abandoned his tribal ways and surrendered himself in Brisbane the day after his sentence was due to expire. However, Brisbane authorities forced him to serve out his full sentence. Because of his knowledge of the Aborigines he was made a 'constable' with some special privileges.

Another convict, David Bracefell, who arrived at Moreton Bay in 1826, escaped four times during what was to have been a fourteen-year sentence. Aborigines named Bracefell *Wandi*, meaning 'The Great Talker'. He first escaped for a month in 1828, voluntarily returned and escaped again for two months in 1829. In 1836, he escaped once more to live with Aborigines but

A Fraser Island Aboriginal man at the turn of the century shows the
ritual scars of manhood. The Kabi were considered a warlike group.

was recaptured in 1837. He escaped yet again in 1839 and remained at large until 1842, when he reluctantly agreed to accompany Andrew Petrie only when assured that Brisbane was no longer a penal settlement and that he no longer faced the lash. Petrie had set out from Brisbane in an open whaleboat to explore the potential of the Moonaboola (now the Mary) River for timber and grazing. On the way he put into what is now Noosa Heads and met Bracefell, who guided him up the Great Sandy Strait to North White Cliffs and over 80 kilometres up the Mary River as far as the rocks at Tiaro.

Near Tiaro Petrie encountered another *bunder*, James Davis, known as *Durrumboi*, who had lived with the Aborigines for fourteen years and was very reluctant to return to the penal settlement. *Durrumboi* and *Wandi* apparently held different tribal or family allegiance. During the voyage back to Brisbane in the crowded boat there was a hostility between the two that almost ended in bloodshed.

Both Davis and Bracefell were free men on their arrival in Brisbane. Davis set up a business there, married and outlived one white wife, remarried and prospered to a ripe old age. He died a wealthy businessman. Except for a few colourful accounts of tribal life within the first few months of his rescue, Davis remained tight-lipped about his years with the Aborigines. Bracefell was signed over to Dr Simpson at Goodna, but was killed not long afterwards when a tree limb fell on him. With him died invaluable recollections of life among the Aboriginal people. However, Bracefell had described some of his recollections to Dr Simpson, who fortunately recorded them. These two ill-educated men, through poorly documented recollections, have provided most of our information on Aboriginal tribal life in the region.

THE DEMISE OF THE ABORIGINES

When the survivors of the wrecked *Stirling Castle* stumbled ashore in the Great Sandy Region in 1836, their European perception of their fate created hostility to the Aborigines. Captain James Fraser was said to have been speared to death by the Aborigines; his first mate, Brown, is alleged to have been burnt at the stake; Eliza Fraser was 'enslaved' in what most Europeans regarded as wretched conditions. That fateful episode was mischievously distorted and led to the beginning of the dispossession of the Aborigines of the region. As Europeans began to take possession of land adjacent to the Great Sandy Region there was intense conflict between Aborigines and settlers and some bloody battles were fought. Thousands of Aborigines were killed in reprisal for the few settlers who died.

Over Christmas 1851, and in the new year period, a motley detachment of native police, squatters, boat crews and others made a murderous raid on the Aborigines of Fraser Island, allegedly to capture some Aborigines who had committed crimes on the mainland and retreated into hiding on the island. The raid was a succession of massacres. A *Moreton Bay Courier* report claimed that 'rumours are afloat that the natives were driven into the sea and there kept as long as daylight or life lasted . . .' and that the 'jaunt . . . by

*T*he Noosa River takes its name from *Ngoothooruo* or *Nuthooroo,* a ghost, or more properly the shade of a tree.

*T*hese satinays have survived the logging which has severely degraded
the forests of the Great Sandy Region. European exploitation of the area's
timber resources had considerable impact on the Aboriginal people.

the most heterogeneous body of black hunters . . . was shrouded with extraordinary secrecy'. Certainly Frederick Walker, the commander of the native
police, provided an improbable alibi for his part when he said that he was
too footsore to pursue the hostile blacks and that he was forced to leave those
under his command to their own devices.

In 1857, the schooner *Seabelle* was lost at sea on a voyage from Glad-
stone to Brisbane and is believed to have foundered off Fraser Island. In 1859,
Brisbane authorities heard rumours that two white girls were living with the
Fraser Island Aborigines. They were believed to be survivors of the *Seabelle*
and a reward was offered to anyone who could bring them back to civilisation. This created an ugly incident in which two albino Aboriginal girls
were forcefully abducted so the 'rescuers' could claim the reward. The girls
suffered agony and grief, fretting away in Sydney before dying prematurely
in institutions. The betrayal of trust resulting from this incident established
a justifiable Aboriginal cynicism towards the new occupiers of the land.

Although in 1860 the whole of Fraser Island had been gazetted as an
Aboriginal reserve, the discovery of extensive stands of valuable commercial
timber two years later by Tom Petrie, the son of Andrew, caused the reverse
to be revoked. The first timber was cut by 'Yankee Jack' Piggott in 1863.
A year later he was speared to death. As this is one of the few violent
confrontations by blacks against whites on Fraser Island, it seems certain that
Piggott had deeply offended the Aborigines. Timber-getting took precedence

*A*borigines knew the kauri pine as *Dundathu.*

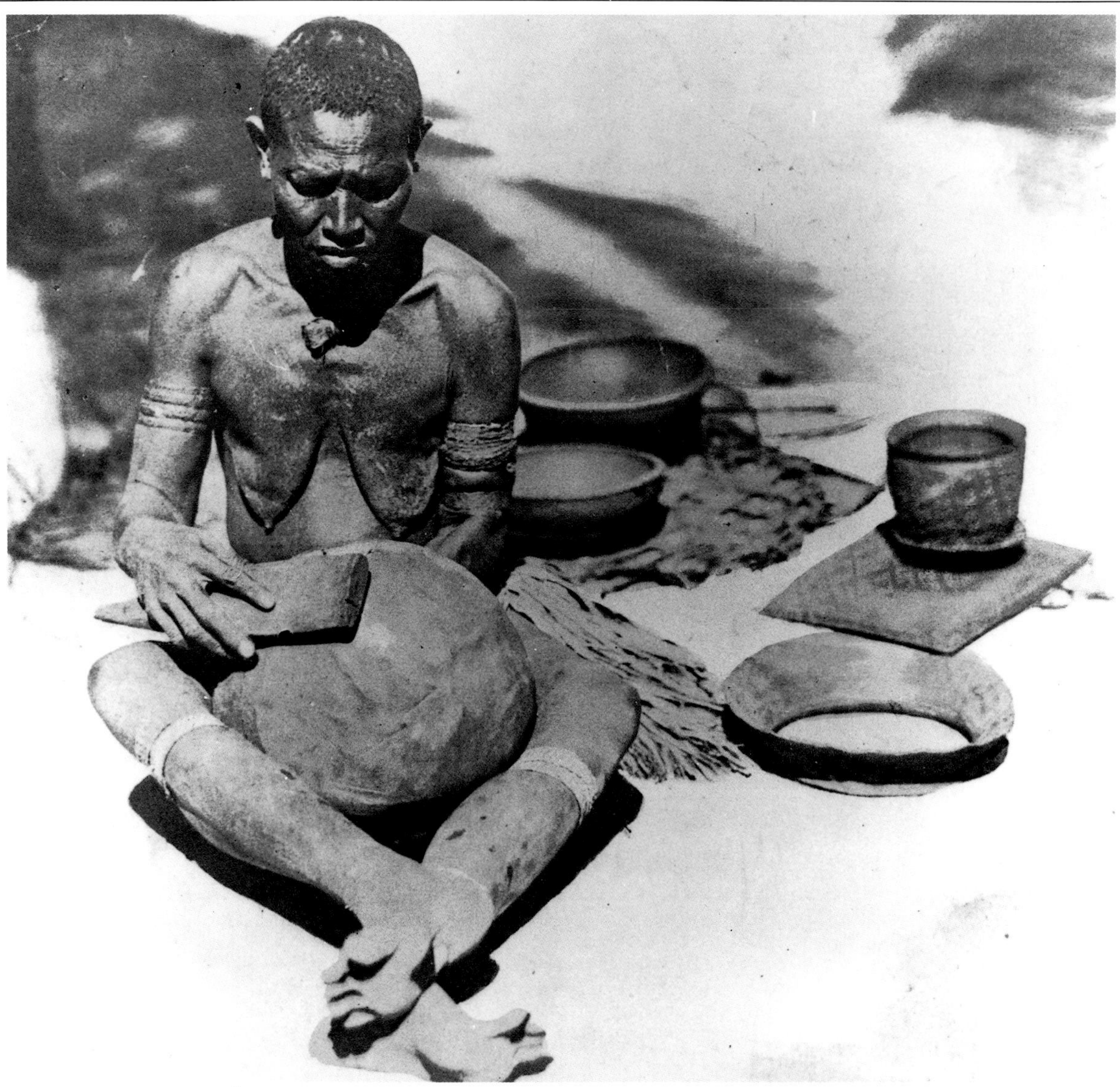

*A*n Aboriginal woman at Central Station. The coming of Europeans
changed forever the lives of the region's Aboriginal community.

over all competing land uses for more than a century, and the demise of the frustrated and disillusioned Aborigines continued with accelerating pace.

Matthew Flinders' report indicates that the Aborigines were numerous at Sandy Cape in August 1802. There were probably even more in the southern area where fresh water was more plentiful. Today there are many more middens in the south. How and why the population declined at Sandy Cape is unclear but it seems likely that the Aborigines there suffered badly at the hands of the whites. Probably, in accordance with the pattern of the times, the Aboriginal population around Rooney Point would have been decimated as a reprisal for the killing of 'Yankee Jack'.

In October 1870, the Reverend William Fuller came to the Great Sandy Region to convert the Aborigines to Christianity. He established his mission at North White Cliffs, an area known to the Aborigines as *Balarrgan*, and important to them as one of the most habitable sites along Great Sandy Strait. Although Balarrgan's historical Aboriginal traditions have been largely lost, some records remain. The Reverend Fuller, for example, reported how in 1870 the residents of his mission would swim out to pilot ships through the strait in return for biscuits and tobacco: 'If a schooner is passing . . . about sunset the natives will sometimes throw sand into the air and blow with their mouths towards the sun in order to make . . . [it] go down quickly and thus compel the schooner to come to anchor for the night . . . to enable them to get on board and obtain tobacco, biscuits, etc. which the Captains generally supply them with.'

Fuller's mission was short-lived and he left for Noosa in 1872. According to official records there were then 171 Aborigines living at, or near, his settlement at North White Cliffs. However, before Fuller left he did establish one historical precedent by being the first white man married on Fraser Island. The Reverend J. Buckle accompanied Miss Winstone to Fraser Island and (as reported by Fuller himself), 'with a minimum of ceremony we changed her name to Fuller'.

From his new base at Noosa, the Reverend Fuller reported an ugly story of the malicious massacre of dozens of innocent blacks at Murdering Creek near Lake Weyba. Many curious Aborigines were lured into a foul trap by murderous pioneers. They followed a man in a small boat until a volley of fire from Europeans lying in ambush turned the quiet creek red with blood.

After Fuller abandoned his mission, Balarrgan was converted into a quarantine station. In early 1897 Archibald Meston, the Protector of Aborigines, established the next Aboriginal settlement at Balarrgan, which he reported was 'a favourite camp for ages'. On 23 February 1897 Meston 'mustered' thirty-three men and boys, and eighteen women and girls. The remnants of the Aboriginal groups from the island and around Maryborough were forced to occupy the deserted buildings of the old quarantine station. By May the number had grown to seventy-three, but Meston's 'musters' soon led to Balarrgan becoming a kind of concentration camp under control of his pugilistic son, Harold. Meston's aim was to muster all Aborigines from the southern Queensland mainland and 'deport' them to Fraser Island. He believed that under proper care and regulation these people would eventually return to the way of life of their ancestors, and wrote:

> I hope within three months to show results that will fully justify the Government Expenditure and the Home Secretary's confidence in myself. The present is the turning point in the history of the Queensland Aboriginal. For the first time since separation, we have a Ministry who are all friendly to the blacks and unanimous in a desire to improve them. If the Fraser Island settlement realises my expectations, it will establish a permanent precedent, and the problem of the future of the Aboriginals will be at last near a satisfactory solution.

A Fraser Island Aborigine poses for the camera in hunting accoutrements.

On 16 April 1897 Aborigines fought off a party of Maryborough excursionists who had landed on the beach at Balarrgan. This led to both a court case and a petition in Maryborough — the first of many collected in that city concerning Fraser Island. Over seven hundred petitioners protested against the establishment of another Aboriginal settlement at White Cliffs, which had been 'a favourite resort for pleasure parties for over 20 years'.

A month later over three hundred people attended a public meeting in Maryborough and claimed White Cliffs as 'their watering place since before Queensland got separation'. They were indignant at having White Cliffs 'wrenched away from them', believing that this was an 'encroachment upon white man's rights to privileges'. The meeting achieved the desired results. Only a week later the Queensland government regazetted White Cliffs as a quarantine station, reversing a forgotten order of 1894 which had made it a recreation reserve.

In this encounter, the Europeans were able to show that their 'favourite resort for pleasure parties for over 20 years' was the basis of a stronger claim to the land in white law than 'a favourite camp for ages' for the Aborigines. The Maryborough residents succeeded in having the Aborigines shifted to Bogimbah. This was not the second preference for either the Aborigines or Archibald Meston, who wanted the settlement moved to Stewart Island.

The Queensland government's policy of ignoring Aboriginal tribal identities, cultural and social practices, and traditional hostilities resulted in the amalgamation of hundreds of Aborigines from all parts of Queensland in one settlement. At one stage nineteen different linguistic groups were represented at Bogimbah. Due to poor management, malnutrition, diseases (including influenza and venereal disease) and drugs (including opium and alcohol) introduced by Europeans, there was an extremely high mortality rate. Within seven years, fifty-six Aborigines were buried in one cemetery and thirty-eight in another.

During the next five years of the Bogimbah settlement, Aborigines lived in abominable conditions. Unknown dozens died of malnutrition, dysentery, syphilis, influenza and tuberculosis. The Anglican missionaries who had taken over Meston's control in 1900 abandoned the settlement in 1904. Driven like cattle by mounted police, some survivors of the mission were transferred to Woodford and later to Cherbourg. Over a hundred of the remaining inmates

*T*his group of Aborigines at Urang Creek in about 1908 includes
'Nugget' (centre), a fine fisherman and friend to European pioneers.

were exiled to Yarrabah near Cairns, 1500 kilometres from their traditional homeland. They were the only remnants of over 2000 Fraser Island Aborigines fifty years earlier. The tragedy prompted one Maryborough resident to write an 'enraged memorial': 'Isn't this one of the blackest pages in the history of the British Empire?'

Rollo Petrie, who grew up with some of the Aborigines who had lived at Bogimbah, has related part of the history of the settlement:

> Meston through the will of the waddy would cure all differences. He handed over to missionaries of three different denominations. Some only stayed a short time. One in particular was responsible for the large death rate and misery towards the closing chapters of the settlement. They were unscrupulous, cruel and dominating. When blacks were taken away, some escaped, some jumped into water. In 1913, a small camp lived in Bogimbah. From there some followed us down to Wanggoolba. Others finished up at Urangan. Old Gindy Simpson, who worked for Mum, was a young lubra during missionary times. She bore the brand of the cat-of-nine-tails on her back. She was flogged for refusing to join the harem of one white missionary. She escaped from the Mission when the Aborigines were moved from the island. Gindy was devoted to my mother. She used to say 'I love you Mrs., I love you Missy'. At the same time she used to tell my mother: 'Never, never walk in front of me, Missy No More'. She couldn't trust herself not to hit a white on the back of the head with a hammer or tomahawk because she had been treated so badly by the missionaries.
>
> One punishment meted out by the missionary was to tie the black to be punished to a tree, then put a length of fuse starting at his feet and laid out several feet. The far end would be lighted. One can imagine the terror it could cause. The blacks had seen dynamite used to blow out stumps, but would at that time not understand the mechanism . . . No doubt some would die or be jibbering idiots afterwards.

Not all the massacres of Aborigines are well documented, but there are substantiated reports of a massacre of Butchalla people on the banks of the Mary River in Maryborough by the black police unit from another tribe before the turn of the century. This matter was hushed up and apparently no punitive action was taken against the offenders. There are also reports of white settlers feeding Aborigines flour laced with arsenic.

The deportation of Fraser Island Aborigines from their tribal territory continued until the 1930s, when 'Banjo' Henry Owens was the last known Butchalla to be sent to Cherbourg under police escort for no criminal offence. Despite the impact on their race, many descendants of the survivors of the missions now live in the Hervey Bay area. The fate of the Noosa blacks seems to have been more complete than their cousins of Fraser Island. In 1894 there were reportedly 700 blacks in the area. Ten years later there were none.

THE ABORIGINAL LEGACY

Little of the culture and history of the Aborigines of the Great Sandy Region is recorded, largely because the early white settlers were contemptuous of their indigenous lifestyle. Within sixty years Aborigines were in turn degraded, debased, detribalised and finally destroyed in an era of ugly unrecorded history. The only visible remnants of the once-rich Aboriginal culture are their middens, canoe and gunyah trees and a few other markings such as scars where bees' nests were removed, which only the astute observer may notice. Many archaeological deposits have fallen victim to thoughtless destruction by visitors, and some were destroyed by sandmining.

Although examination of the archaeological potential of the region has been restricted, a number of sites have been located, particularly adjacent to the eastern shore and some active sandblows. One extensive site stretched for a considerable distance inland from the coast at the mouth of Bogimbah Creek. It is expected that further important sites will be discovered as more archaeological survey work is carried out. Dr Peter Lauer, curator of the Anthropology Museum at the University of Queensland, who has done extensive archaeological work on both Fraser Island and Lake Mungo, one of Australia's most famous Aboriginal sites, claims that, based on the number of artefacts on Fraser Island, the Great Sandy Region is archaeologically at least as significant as Lake Mungo.

Over two hundred shell middens have been found on Fraser Island, and 102 have been recorded in Cooloola. They are almost exclusively composed

*A*boriginal shell middens provide valuable evidence of the lives of the region's earliest inhabitants. However, damage by erosion is a constant problem.

*A*boriginal stone implements are continually being
exposed in sandblows by erosion.

*T*he shells of a bivalve mollusc *Plebidonax deltoides,* known to the Butchalla as *ah-wong,* occur frequently in Aboriginal middens. Once exposed, the old shells quickly disintegrate.

*T*hese two clay pipes, of a type used for trading by seventeenth century Dutch navigators, were discovered in a midden.

of eugaries (*Plebidonax deltoides*). Two clay pipes of a type used for trading by seventeenth century Dutch navigators were also found in the middens. Along the west coast of Fraser Island are a number of archaeological sites, of which more than thirty have been recorded. Middens also line the shores of Tin Can Bay, and are found on some of the islands within the Great Sandy Strait. These estuary middens are composed mainly of oyster shells (*Ostreidae* sp.) and whelks (*Pyrazus ebeninus*).

Apart from the middens, artefacts of stone constitute the only recoverable cultural materials. Seventeen kinds of stone implements have been recognised. The most common of these are scrapers, knives, cores, choppers, pebble scrapers, hammerstones, points, axes, adzes, mullers, polishing stones, an anvil and a whetstone. To date, pebble scrapers and choppers have not been identified from any other region in Australia. Because it was naturally hardened by silicification, chert is an ideal material for making stone tools. It is of sedimentary origin, deposited under shallow water conditions believed to be of the Cretaceous age. This rock occurs at Boon Boon Creek, and is exposed on Big Woody Island in the Great Sandy Strait. Outcrops occur on other parts of the Maryborough formation.

On Big Woody Island, eleven oyster shell middens and a large stone-walled tidal fishtrap on the western shore have been identified. No actual quarry sites have been located, but the most frequently formed artefacts were made of the stone that occurs on the island. It is possible that some of the rocks used for stone tools have come from deposits now below sea level which were quarried when the sea levels were much lower. Some stone may have been introduced from other regions through trading.

Other anthropological relics to be observed in the Great Sandy Region include gunyah trees (trees stripped of a section of bark to provide a roof for a dwelling), canoe trees, and trees that have been robbed of native bees' honey. A number of camping and ceremonial sites (bora rings) have been

*T*he estuarine middens of the Great Sandy Strait are made up largely
of the shells of oysters and whelks.

identified throughout the region, although many of these have been inadvertently disturbed or destroyed since European settlement. Other sites have been entombed by advancing sandblows. Many of today's vehicular tracks in the Great Sandy Region follow ancient Aboriginal footpaths.

ABORIGINAL PLACE NAMES

In 1978, responding to Aboriginal concern that so many ancient place names had been redesignated by European settlers, the Queensland Place Names Board reinstated a number of Aboriginal place names on Fraser Island. Where the original names could not be traced, new but appropriate Aboriginal names were applied. In a further effort to preserve Aboriginal nomenclature, the spelling of some names, such as Lake Boomanjin, Wanggoolba and Boon Boon creeks, was changed to make them closer phonetically to the local Aboriginal pronunciation.

An absurdity of European nomenclature was the naming of four major creeks just south of Eurong which had been unimaginatively called First, Second, Third and Fourth creeks. The Aboriginal names have now been reinstated: First Creek became *Gerawwea* (meaning flying fox); Second Creek became *Govi* (native bee); Third Creek became *Taleeba* (a vine); Fourth Creek became *Tooloora* (a louse).

Although Sandy Cape retained the name given to it by Cook in 1770, the Aboriginal name *Carree* is applied to the parish in which it stands. The lighthouse stands on a hill known to Aborigines as *Wocco* (meaning mopoke). Indian Head, which rises to a height of 60 metres, was known to the Aborigines as *Tuckee* (stone) or *Walarr* (basalt). Waddy Point is a name of unknown origin; it was known to Aborigines as *Binngih*. Although the meanings of names for many lakes such as Coomboo, Garawongera, Boomanjin and Benaroon have been lost, the original Aboriginal names have been retained. Even the Anglicised name Garrys Camp comes from Garry Owens, a well-known Aboriginal tracker, whose name was probably derived either from *Kgari*, the Aboriginal name for Fraser Island, or from *Gurree*, the local name for man.

Many places in the Cooloola area have Aboriginal names. Tin Can, despite its anglicised connotation, is derived from *Tinchin*, or *Tindhin*, the Aborigines' name for a species of mangrove; Mudlo Rocks at Rainbow Beach comes from *Mudlu*, meaning a stone; Tewantin is derived from *dauwa* (dead logs) and *dhan* (place of) — a reference to Pettigrew's sawmill; Noosa is evidently a corrupted Aboriginal word thought to be *Ngoothooruo* or *Nuthooroo*, meaning a ghost, or more properly the shade of a tree — an appropriate name for the river which is almost completely shaded by trees.

A number of Aborigines living in the Hervey Bay area are descended from Fraser Island Aborigines. They have formed the Butchalla Association and have secured a small area of land on Fraser Island where they are developing the Thoorgine Educational and Cultural Centre. This is planned as the repository for preserved archaeological relics and a place where Aborigines can rekindle their lost culture.

*T*o the Aborigines, *Birrabeen* was the name for a macrozamia. It now applies to a perched lake of crystal clear water.

*C*ooloola is derived from the Aboriginal word for cypress pine. The area
has a complex and significant Aboriginal history.

EXPLORERS AND SETTLERS

After more than 40 000 years, Aboriginal culture was disturbed, at first by a few Europeans arriving by ship, and from 1830 by a land-based invasion. The first strangers in foreign ships arrived 500 years ago, 250 years before Captain Cook sailed the shores of the Great Sandy Region.

There is evidence that Portuguese explorers discovered Fraser Island as early as the fifteenth century. Christado de Mendonca explored the east Australian coast in 1521, and Portuguese charts published in 1536 clearly show a large island along the east coast of *Terra Australis*. Despite the distortions resulting from poor navigational instruments and strange projections, this island corresponds with the position of Fraser Island, and the map indicates that Fraser Island was sufficiently well explored by the Portuguese to be identified as an island. British navigators did not establish that Fraser Island was an island until 1824.

To add to this intrigue, Bill Ward, a soil scientist, established that a piece of lead he discovered on the southern end of Fraser Island in 1986 had been deposited there in about 1450. By some incredible forensic work he identified the lead as coming from a mine at Rio Tinto in southern Spain. The Portuguese kept their discoveries secret because of their rivalry with Spain and because the Pope had decreed that this part of the globe should be Spanish territory.

Though copies of the charts were smuggled out of Lisbon, most of the original material was lost in a Lisbon earthquake in 1755. It is thought, however, that the British had obtained copies of the records and that these

Sunset silhouettes Great Sandy Strait mangroves at Hook Point.

The dramatic and beautiful Fraser Island coastline.

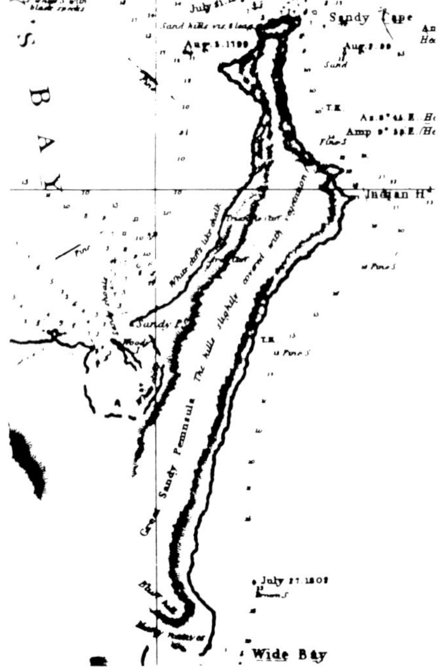

formed the basis of secret orders given to Captain Cook when he left on his round-the-world expedition in 1769. There is evidence too that Dutch navigators had followed the Portuguese before Captain Cook and made undocumented visits to the Great Sandy Region. Two clay pipes of a type used exclusively by seventeenth century Dutch navigators to trade with indigenous people have been discovered in middens near Indian Head.

Three English Navigators

The written history of the region has been closely documented only since Captain Cook's voyage in the *Endeavour*. On 19 May 1770 he named Double Island Point 'on account of its figure'. Cook also named as Wide Bay the big sweep north of Double Island Point and noted that 'The land within this Point itself is of moderate and pretty equal height, but the Point itself is of such an unequal height that it looks like two small islands lying under the land; it likewise may be known by the white cliffs on the north side of it'. The following day, Cook through his telescope 'saw several people upon the shore'. Aborigines seeking a better view of the *Endeavour* had assembled there. Because Europeans regarded all indigenous people as 'Indians', Cook forthwith named the locality 'Indian Head'.

The next record of exploration was that of Matthew Flinders, who sailed these waters in the 16-ton ship *Norfolk*. He became the first recorded white man to land on Fraser Island and to sail into Hervey Bay. Flinders first visited Sandy Cape on 1 August 1799. He then sailed down Hervey Bay and named features such as Triangle and Arch Cliffs, Sandy Point and White Cliffs. According to his journal, he 'entertained a conjecture that the Head of Hervey's Bay might communicate with Wide Bay'. Flinders was prevented from sailing up the Great Sandy Strait by the mud-banks and tortuous shallows and was thus unable to prove his theory.

Three years later, in 1802, Flinders returned aboard the *Investigator*, and later still recorded his observations of the Cooloola coast in *A Voyage to Terra Australis*. On 27 July he sailed between Double Island Point and Wolf Rock. On his charts he noted on Teewah beach: 'Front ridges of barren sandy land', and on Rainbow beach, those magnificent variegated curtains of sand, he labelled 'White Sandy Cliffs'. Flinders had a rendezvous with a supply ship, the *Lady Nelson*, at Sandy Cape. He had no time to spare, nor could he take foolhardy risks, so he was not able to explore the opening of the head of the

*M*atthew Flinders' chart of what he called the Great Sandy Peninsula (above) and William Westall's sketch of the coastline (right) were published in *A Voyage to Terra Australis* in 1814.

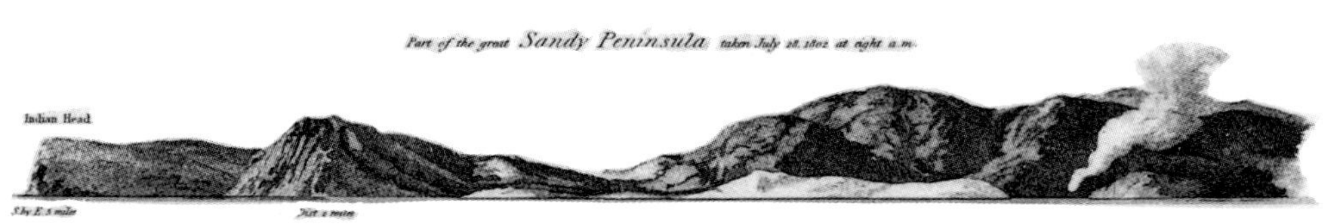

*I*ndian Head was named by Captain Cook on 20 May 1770 because
through his telescope he 'saw several people upon the shore'. Aborigines,
whom Europeans patronisingly named 'Indians', had assembled there.

Great Sandy Strait. His observations about Cooloola proved accurate in all respects except for the colour of the sand. He did not seem any more excited about Fraser Island's appearance than Captain Cook, noting:

> This part of the coast is very barren; there being great patches of movable sand many acres in extent through which appeared in some places the green tops of grass, half buried, and in others the naked trunks of such as the sand has destroyed . . . Nothing can be imagined more barren than this peninsula, but the smoke which arose in many parts corroborated [estimates of a 'more numerous population of Indians than is usual to the Southward'] and bespoke that fresh water was not scarce in this Sandy Country: Our course at night was directed by the fires on shore. . . .

Flinders went on to Bool Creek, near where the Sandy Cape lighthouse now stands, and landed three parties. One group collected firewood, another of six naturalists under botanist Robert Brown studied the flora, while Flinders befriended the Aborigines, whom he considered numerous and of good physique. Brown collected a species of dogwood which he named *Jacksonia*. His descriptions provide the earliest scientific records from Fraser Island.

Twenty years later Captain William Edwardson proved that Flinders' conjecture that the Great Sandy peninsula was an island was indeed true. Sent by Governor Brisbane in the cutter *Snapper* to locate a river location suitable for a new penal settlement, Edwardson sailed up the Great Sandy Strait. He failed to discover the Mary River and assumed that Tin Can Bay was a river. Although Edwardson described the strait as 'a safe and capacious anchorage', his report did not influence the siting of a new settlement. That was accomplished in 1824, when colonial authorities in Sydney ordered the establishment of the Moreton Bay penal settlement.

ELIZA FRASER

Having taken its cargo from London to Van Diemen's Land, the 500-ton brig *Stirling Castle* was returning to London in ballast via Sydney, Singapore and the Torres Straits. On the night of 22 May 1836, the ship struck a coral reef hundreds of kilometres north of Fraser Island and was wrecked. There were eighteen people aboard, including Captain James Fraser's heavily pregnant wife, Eliza.

After some initial confusion, the crew managed to launch a longboat and the ship's pinnace. A course was set towards the nearest European settlement at Moreton Bay, over 1000 kilometres to the south. The stronger men manned the longboat which towed the pinnace carrying the less able, including the sickly Captain Fraser and his wife. Towing the pinnace slowed the longboat's progress, so one night the desperate rowers cut the pinnace adrift. Subsequently, the longboat crew landed on what is now the Gold Coast. They started a futile walk south from which only one survived.

Those manning the pinnace kept well to the seaward for fear of the Aborigines along the coast. During the six weeks in the pinnace, Eliza Fraser gave birth to a child, which survived only a few hours. The crew, in need of drinking water, landed in the vicinity of Waddy Point, Fraser Island, where they abandoned the unseaworthy pinnace on 26 June 1836.

Crowds of excited, chattering Aborigines surrounded the exhausted, extremely sunburnt survivors. Captain Fraser and his crew were stripped of their clothes and taken away. They suffered unaccustomed hardship. Mrs Fraser was left alone overnight on the windswept beach. In the morning she was taken by the Aboriginal women to their camp, where she found her husband and his companions.

Eliza Fraser subsisted with the Aborigines for seven weeks until 17 August. She was required to do what any Aboriginal woman would do: dig roots, find food and firewood, and live a spartan existence. It obviously did not satisfy her. In a later narrative of her 'captivity' she described her hardships:

> During the whole of my detention among the natives I was treated with the greatest cruelty, being obliged to fetch wood and water for them and constantly beaten when incapable of carrying the heavy loads they put upon me; exposed during the night to the inclemency of the weather, being hardly ever allowed to enter their huts even during the heaviest rain.

*E*liza Fraser was shipwrecked near Waddy Point in 1836. After spending seven weeks with the Aborigines she was rescued from Cooloola near Elanda Point.

Her accounts were doubtlessly embellished as she travelled in both Australia and Britain earning money and fame by recounting her 'ordeal'.

Half the survivors of the pinnace decided to leave the sickly Captain and Mrs Fraser behind. They walked down the beaches as far as Bribie Island, where they met some Moreton Bay settlers who were hunting game there. When word reached Brisbane that there were survivors of the *Stirling Castle* and that Eliza Fraser was in Aboriginal hands, an urgent rescue operation was launched. That rescue revealed a rich new territory which was coveted ever after by the Europeans.

From here on the story of Eliza Fraser is inextricably bound up with the story of the 'white blackfellows', particularly the literate convicts John Graham and David Bracefell. Although the credit for bringing Mrs Fraser back is officially given to Graham, many believe that Bracefell played the major part.

The rescue was undertaken by a party led by Lieutenant Otter. Three days after word reached Brisbane, Otter and Graham set out in a longboat. They camped at Noosa Heads, where they recovered two more of the crew, and then set out on a futile trek along Teewah beach, trying to find clues to Mrs Fraser's whereabouts. By this time, Mrs Fraser had been transported from Fraser Island across Cooloola to Lake Cootharaba where a big corroboree was under way. She was the prize exhibit.

Graham set off from Double Island Point alone and unarmed, and learnt that Mrs Fraser, 'the She Ghost', was at the corroboree ground near Lake Cootharaba. Baxter, the other survivor, was on the southern end of Fraser Island. Graham first made a daring solo rescue of Baxter by crossing from Inskip Point in a commandeered less-than-seaworthy canoe at the wrong time of the tide. He then set off to recover Mrs Fraser. He walked some 50 kilometres down Teewah beach across the dunes and waded through the swamps to the edges of Lake Cootharaba.

Fortunately, the belief in reincarnation, which had helped so many *bunders* to survive with the Aborigines, helped the rescue. Graham convinced his former stepsons and his father-in-law that Mrs Fraser was the reincarnation of his long-dead former wife, and persuaded the Aborigines not only to release Eliza Fraser, but to convey her by canoe across the lake. They then escorted her to a waterhole where they waited until he returned with suitable clothing and an escort back to civilisation. The rescue occurred fifty-three days after the pinnace landed on Fraser Island. Graham maximised his role in the rescue in order to obtain the pardon which he was ultimately, but reluctantly, awarded.

There are three versions of the death of Captain Fraser. The first was given by Mrs Fraser just after her rescue. She described the physical hardships he endured, the cruelty with which he was treated and the subsistence diet of 'a small portion of fish which we but very seldom got' and 'a kind of fern root which we were obliged to procure ourselves in the swamps', and continued:

*T*he death of Captain Fraser as conceptualised by Sidney Nolan in one
of the famous paintings from his Eliza Fraser series. There is some doubt
of the veracity of Eliza Fraser's account of her husband's death.

*T*he title page of John Curtis's book indicates the sensationalism that characterised Eliza Fraser's narrative as she capitalised on her ordeal on Fraser Island.

SHIPWRECK

OF THE

STIRLING CASTLE,

CONTAINING

A FAITHFUL NARRATIVE OF THE DREADFUL SUFFERINGS OF THE CREW,

AND THE

CRUEL MURDER OF CAPTAIN FRASER

BY THE SAVAGES.

ALSO,

THE HORRIBLE BARBARITY OF THE CANNIBALS INFLICTED UPON

THE CAPTAIN'S WIDOW,

WHOSE UNPARALLELED SUFFERINGS ARE STATED BY HERSELF, AND CORROBORATED BY THE OTHER SURVIVORS.

TO WHICH IS ADDED,

THE NARRATIVE OF THE WRECK OF THE

CHARLES EATON,

IN THE SAME LATITUDE.

Embellished with Engravings, Portraits, and Scenes illustrative of the Narrative.

By JOHN CURTIS.

LONDON:

PUBLISHED BY GEORGE VIRTUE, IVY LANE,

AND SOLD BY ALL BOOKSELLERS.

M.DCCC.XXXVIII.

In consequence of these hardships my husband soon became so much weakened as to be totally incapable of doing the work that was required of him, and being on one occasion unable through debility to carry a large log of wood, one of the natives threw a spear at him which entered his shoulder a little below the blade bone. Of this wound he never recovered and being soon after seized with a spitting of blood, he gradually pined away until his death which took place eight or nine days afterwards.

The second account was a sensationalised and embellished elaboration of the spearing incident which appeared in a magazine about eighteen months later. The reality was probably more accurately stated by crewman Harry Voulden after his rescue on Bribie Island: 'Boats were sent down the coast for the rest of the long-boat party. When found, the captain and chief-mate were dead. Both had perished of starvation.'

The true circumstances of the whole episode are obscured by Mrs Fraser's conflicting accounts of what did happen during those seven weeks with the tribe. She did not appear to let the truth stand between herself and a good yarn, especially as the good yarn became very profitable after she returned to England in 1837 and gained celebrity status. While Eliza Fraser was fortunate to survive, the Aborigines undoubtedly suffered from the worldwide hostility towards them promoted by her colourful and inventive stories. The lives of the Fraser Island Aborigines changed irrevocably after the survivors of the *Stirling Castle* stumbled ashore.

THE BEGINNINGS OF EUROPEAN SETTLEMENT

In 1842, in order to attract more settlers to substantiate British territorial claims in Queensland, the Moreton Bay penal settlement was closed and the land opened up for free white settlement.

One of the first Europeans to explore the potential of the territory was Andrew Petrie, one-time Superintendent of Public Works in the Brisbane penal colony. With Henry Stuart Russell, Petrie set out to explore the Moonaboola River region, which he had heard of from the Aborigines. On the way he collected the elusive Bracefell, who was living with the Noosa Aborigines and who guided Petrie through the region. After discovering good land and recovering James Davis at Tiaro, Petrie's party returned south, camping near Snout Point on Fraser Island. His was the first recorded party of white men to camp voluntarily on the island.

In 1847 surveyor Burnett selected a township site on the Wide Bay River and in the following year a settlement was begun at Baddow (now a suburb of Maryborough). Governor Fitzroy of the New South Wales colony ordered that the Wide Bay River be renamed the 'Mary' after his wife, who had been tragically killed in her carriage at Parramatta. The settlement grew quickly after gold was discovered at Gympie in 1867. To handle the stream of immigrants to the goldfields, Fraser Island became a quarantine and immigration station. The European population of the district expanded rapidly, serviced almost entirely through the port of Maryborough.

In addition to carrying regional traffic to and from the goldfields, the Great Sandy Strait became a major channel for international shipping. Because of the advantageous winds, sailing vessels from Sydney to London preferred to travel via Singapore. Rather than deviate 80 kilometres into Moreton Bay and up the Brisbane River, many of the ships would drop their Queensland cargo at North White Cliffs and proceed to Torres Strait through Hervey Bay. Maryborough merchants would meet passing international merchant traders at Fraser Island to barter for goods. Ships replenished their drinking water supplies from easily accessible streams on Fraser Island. The seamen on the merchant vessels left behind disease and corruption as well as their wares.

In the 1860s the first livestock were taken to Fraser Island. Three small freehold areas a kilometre north of the 'White Cliffs' were selected in 1880, and in the following year one of Maryborough's pioneers, Harry Aldridge, obtained leases at Eurong and Indian Head. During the drought years between 1901 and 1903, 150 cattle and an unknown number of sheep were loaded on to punts at Mary River heads and towed to Yankee Jack's Creek. The stock remained on the island for nearly two years. Fifteen shearers were brought to shear the sheep at a lake about 24 kilometres from Yankee Jack's Creek, and forty-five bales of wool were hauled to the mainland by bullock wagon. The name 'Sheep Station Lagoons' is a relic of this period of temporary occupation.

Although graziers were seeking pastoral interests on Fraser Island, the timber interests were also quickly entrenched. By 1899 timber operations had precedence over all other land uses on the island. By 1907 these timber interests were limited to two large Maryborough sawmillers. Since then they have vigorously (and so far successfully) fended off threats from rival sawmillers and conservationists who want the island created a national park.

THE TIMBER INDUSTRY

In 1842 Andrew Petrie reported on Fraser Island's superb timber:

> In this scrub I found a species of pine not known before. It is similar
> to the New Zealand cowrie [kauri] pine and bears a cone. It forms
> valuable timber. The Blacks make their nets of the inner bark of this
> tree . . . the formations and productions of the island are much the same
> as those of Moreton Island; the timber is a great deal superior, and also
> the soil; the cypress pine upon Fraser Island being quite splendid.

By 1866 the scrubs of Kin Kin were being felled and taken down to Lake Cootharaba at Elanda Point to be milled and shipped off to Brisbane and Sydney. After the discovery of gold in the following year, the booming Gympie settlement demanded more timber and in 1869 150 timber cutters began a mill to cut pit props for the mines. Other sawmills were established at Tewantin and Colloy on the north shore. In 1877 John Ramsay, who extracted timber from what is now known as Ramsays Scrub, settled a block on the sandmass. He hauled logs by bullock teams to the Noosa River, from where the timber was either punted or rafted to Cootharaba.

One of the relics of the timber industry is the jetty at Mill Point on
Lake Cootharaba, from which timber was exported to Brisbane and
Sydney from 1866. The mill closed after a boiler burst and a number of
workers were killed.

At the same time, Maryborough timber interests were making heavy assaults on the northern end of the Cooloola sandmass. Timber was extracted from Searys Scrub, and teams also worked in Carland Creek (known as Store Creek because its steep sides acted as a wharf for unloading stores) at the head of Tin Can Bay.

In 1873 Pettigrew and Sim constructed at Cooloola the first private railway in Queensland. For eleven years this took timber from Broutha Scrub north to Poverty Point on the shores of Tin Can Inlet. The locomotive *Mary Ann* was the first ever built in Queensland. The rails were of spotted gum, set into slots in cypress pine sleepers held together with wedges. Bullock teams were used in conjunction with the wooden rail tramway. Protected by the damp rainforest, the remains of these rails can still be seen today some 10 kilometres from the terminus at Poverty Point. Some of the cuttings and embankments once used by the railway, a few hundred metres east of Camp Milo, are still in use. Logs from Cooloola continued to be rafted from Tin Can Bay up Sandy Strait to Maryborough until the 1930s.

By 1887 the timber industry was looking far afield for markets. Sleepers were taken to North White Cliffs and loaded on to ships for the new rail line from Darwin. In 1905 cutting of big stands of tallowwood and black-butt in the Poyungan and Bogimbah creek areas began, coinciding with the closure of the Aboriginal mission at Bogimbah Creek. These stands were almost exhausted by 1915. Until then the timber was formed into large rafts

*L*ogs from both Fraser Island and Cooloola were formed into large rafts and floated up the Mary River to the sawmills in Maryborough.

*F*rom 1873 until 1935 steam locomotives hauled logs from the tall forests in the heart of Fraser Island and Cooloola, to be taken across the water in rafts or by punts for processing.

and floated up the Mary River to the sawmills in Maryborough. However, as the denser hardwoods were harvested, techniques changed and the timber was punted in barges. In 1915 the tramline was shifted to tap the Wanggoolba Creek hardwood stands. Logging of the west coast forests, including large cypress to 2.5 metres in diameter, was carried out between Yankee Jack and Bowarrady creeks.

Cooloola was declared a forestry reserve in 1881, and since then the harvest of timber from the area has been substantially reduced. After the Aborigines were removed from Fraser Island, the remnant Aboriginal reserve was revoked in 1906. In 1908 the central part of Fraser Island was declared a forestry reserve, and in 1913 forest ranger Walter Petrie established the first Forestry Department camp at Dipuying, on Bogimbah Creek. By 1925 most of the island had been set aside as state forest.

Petrie was a competent professional forester who, after his service on Fraser Island, became Deputy State Forester for Queensland in 1920. He wrote a number of reports which indicate not only the size of the forest giants but also the rapacious exploitation of the early timber getters:

> In 1913, when I visited the various sites of old operations, a few rotting stumps and tops were to be seen but the positions of the old giants were mostly to be located by the holes left in the ground where the stumps had long since rotted away. Exceptions were the abandoned logs which had become embedded in the sand under the shallow water of the creeks and thus preserved to water level. Exploitation had been heavy and I could see that it would be many a long year before a general logging could be resumed.

With the end of the First World War, things really began to move again around North White Cliffs. The *Brisbane Courier* of 4 July 1918 reported that Mr H. McKenzie, a large New South Wales timber merchant, had contracted to purchase timber from about 10 000 acres (4000 hectares) of Fraser Island. The contract provided for the cutting and sawing of 100 000 super feet (250 cubic metres) a month from April 1919, with a complete removal in ten years. The sawmill was built near the quarantine station, three kilometres inland up Foulmouth Creek (the creek was named for the bad language used at the camp). Although the Maryborough sawmillers logged only tallow-wood and blackbutt, McKenzie's also took satinay and brushbox. The tramline route built to service the sawmill can still be easily traced, with its smooth grades and steep cuttings. It followed a steady climb from the sawmill all the way to the 720 Mark, from which the main line extended east towards Wabby Lakes and Bill Seelke's Camp where the log hauler was located. When McKenzie's sawmill and jetty were abandoned in 1925, the Department of Forestry continued to operate the tramline until 1935.

The postwar building boom and the shortage of building material, plus new technology for kiln drying to prevent scrub timbers from warping, caused a review of earlier prejudice against logging satinay and brushbox. Satinay then won world renown for its straight cylindrical trunks over 30

*G*iant satinays, *peebung* to Aborigines and *Syncarpia hillii* to scientists,
reach a diameter of over 3 metres after 1000 years of growth in the forests
of the Great Sandy Region.

*L*ogging in 1908, probably in the Bogimbah area where a tramline was
first used on Fraser Island to haul timber to the coast.

metres in length, which were found to be resistant to the attacks of marine worms. It has consequently been in great demand for piles for wharves. Fraser Island satinay has in fact been used in London's Tilbury docks and timber from Fraser Island was used for sidings in the Suez Canal.

The first detailed timber resource survey of Fraser Island was made in 1920. By 1948 70 per cent of the previously estimated timber reserves had been removed. There have been two detailed inventories since then, in 1958 and 1977. Since 1968 the annual removal of forest timber from Fraser Island has averaged 21 000 cubic metres. Selection and marketing of the standing trees is today controlled by the Forestry Department which has a very small workforce of fewer than ten men on Fraser Island. This group also maintains fire control, regeneration and silvicultural treatment of the island's forests, as well as managing the recreational use of the parts of Fraser Island under its jurisdiction.

Currently, Fraser Island logs are processed in Maryborough or Urangan. The timber is collected from punting log dumps on tidal creeks between Moon Point and Fig Tree and is taken by barge up the Mary River. Only one logging contractor now handles all timber extraction, and mechanisation of the industry has dramatically reduced the number of employees. Timber interests have opposed all attempts to make the whole of the Great Sandy Region a national park. This has resulted in the Cooloola National Park being 'the park with a hole in the heart' or 'the doughnut' to yield a mere 2267 cubic metres of commercial timber per annum.

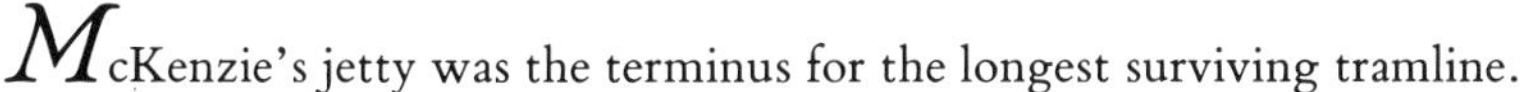

*M*cKenzie's jetty was the terminus for the longest surviving tramline.

POSTWAR DEVELOPMENTS

The tranquillity of isolation was shattered by the Second World War. An airstrip was built near Rooney Point and a radar station near the Sandy Cape lighthouse. The war brought one of Australia's most famous military commando units, Z Force, to Fraser Island. Hundreds camped near McKenzie's jetty at Balarrgan or North White Cliffs and Lake McKenzie, training for some of the most successful raids of the war. Curiously, their camp had been the site of the first mission station, quarantine station, forestry headquarters and trading centres.

After the war, events rapidly overtook Fraser Island. Spurred by the postwar building boom, forestry officers changed their approach to maximise timber production. Tourism developed very slowly until 1963, when a new village was surveyed and subdivided at Eurong. Happy Valley was expanded and Orchid Beach Tourist Resort was established. The infant tourist industry was boosted following the establishment in 1970 of a vehicular ferry service at Inskip Point by Gordon Elmer. Today three ferry services operate from the mainland across to Fraser Island.

In 1948 geological surveys had established the existence of commercial rutile and zircon deposits on Fraser Island, and private mining operations commenced on Teewah beach. In 1963 multinational companies made the first substantial move to mine areas of Fraser Island above the high water mark. Mining began at Inskip Point in 1966, and on Fraser Island in 1971. Sandmining had ceased at Cooloola and on Fraser Island by December 1976, with less than 1000 hectares affected. In 1964, six exploratory oil wells were drilled along Teewah and Cooloola beaches. On Fraser Island, seismic surveys were carried out during the 1960s, as part of an ongoing oil exploration program. A bore hole was drilled by the Queensland Mines Department in 1980 at Sandy Cape, to extract stratigraphic information.

SHIPWRECKS AND LIGHTHOUSES

There have been a large number of shipwrecks in the vicinity of the Great Sandy Region especially on the sandy shoals of the treacherous Wide Bay bar and Breaksea Spit, a formidable shipping obstacle. The remains of some of these wrecks are in evidence along the coasts of Cooloola (*Cherry Venture*, 1973) and Fraser Island (*Marloo*, 1914; *Maheno*, 1935).

In 1864 the American sailing ship *Panama* hit Breaksea Spit and was beached at Rooney Point. The passengers and some of the crew camped on the beach but returned to the ship when twelve Aborigines entered the camp at night and took all their goods. Later 200 Aborigines tried to get on board but were bluffed by the sailors' cutlasses. The captain and seven of the crew escaped in a lifeboat and were picked up near Woody Island. The Aborigines later brought 'fine big fish' and held a corroboree on the spot, but did not attack again. The skeleton of a ship, presumed to be the *Panama*, could clearly be seen offshore at Rooney Point in 1948.

*T*he Sandy Cape lighthouse sits atop a ridge 7 kilometres from the shoals of Breaksea Spit.

*T*he steamer *Maheno,* built in Scotland in 1905, broke loose during a
July cyclone in 1935 while being towed to be scrapped in Japan.

In 1884 the *Chang Chow* was smashed as it tried to navigate the shoals of Sandy Cape near Breaksea Spit. The ship was laden with Chinese miners returning to their homeland from the goldfields. Some of the crew walked 60 kilometres to a timber getter's camp and were taken from there by tug to the telegraph station at Woody Island. Eventually, all were rescued. In 1904, the *Aramac* bumped hard several times on Breaksea Spit. After 24 kilometres the ship was leaking badly. The crew and passengers took to the boats and safely reached Burnett Head and Baffle Point. The captain and six men remained on board and finally succeeded in anchoring the *Aramac* in the protection of Platypus Bay.

In 1905 the anchor of the *Waiwera*, a bêche-de-mer schooner, gave way and the ship came to grief on Breaksea Spit. The captain, his son and six of the crew rowed the lifeboat for forty hours, without food or drink, to reach Waddy Point, 45 kilometres away. The rest of the crew escaped in dinghies and walked around to Rooney Point. In 1914 the *Marloo*, a luxury Italian liner, bumped hard on Sandy Cape shoal in calm weather. The ship was beached and help was sought from Sandy Cape lighthouse. The beach was strewn with green tomatoes and bottles of whisky.

The most famous wreck was that of the 5323-ton triple-screw steamer *Maheno*, which broke loose during a July cyclone in 1935 while being towed to be scrapped in Japan. Launched in Scotland in 1905, the *Maheno* was used

*T*he *Cherry Venture* was wrecked in 1973. Despite attempts to salvage the freighter, it is now a rusting landmark on Teewah beach.

as a trans-Tasman liner until patronage declined in the 1930s. The Japanese put considerable effort into trying to refloat the disabled hulk and to charting much of Fraser Island, which later played a conspicuous part in Japan's invasion plans of Australia.

The saga of the *Cherry Venture* began in an unseasonable cyclone in July 1973. In the furious seas the hapless ship, bound from Sydney to Singapore, without any cargo or ballast, faced an impossible task. After a valiant fight the small ship lost its rudder, surrendered to the conquering seas and was driven ashore, to be stranded on Teewah beach, 3 kilometres south of the lighthouse, on 8 July. Salvage hunters, sensing a potential bonanza, purchased the ship from the insurance brokers, with an inflexible obligation to remove the marooned freighter, either by refloating it or by breaking it up for scrap metal. There followed a four-year struggle to free the stranded freighter from the sucking sand, during which a series of frustrating misadventures thwarted the refloating efforts as success was almost within the salvagers' grasp. Finally recognising that refloating was impossible, the salvagers took what they could and abandoned the rest to become an ugly landmark on Teewah beach.

The Sandy Cape lighthouse was first recommended in 1864 by a select committee in a report to the Queensland Legislative Council. Despite the urgency of the committee's recommendation, tenders did not close until four years later. The successful tender was for 4524 pounds to build the 30-metre-tall iron tower which had been manufactured in Bridgewater, England. The tapered sections were landed at Panama Point and the parts hauled by bullocks along the beach and up the 100-metre elevated ridge where the sections, made with such precision, were bolted together.

The light was first exhibited on 19 May 1870, and has continued to function continuously for over a century, although it has been converted from kerosene to electricity. The 120-volt 1000-watt quartz iodide tungsten halogen light is magnified by the prisms to an intensity of half a million candles. It is visible for 44 kilometres to sea, although the loom is visible for more than 80 kilometres on a clear night. The light flashes at precisely ten second intervals.

One interesting aspect of the operations of the Sandy Cape lighthouse has been the strenuous and innovative efforts to maintain communications between Sandy Cape and the mainland. A telegraph line had been built from Hervey Bay to Sandy Cape by the turn of the century. A submarine cable ran from Urangan to Woody Island, before running down the length of Woody Island, then across to Bogimbah. From here a resident line keeper patrolled the line. For several years Pat Seary maintained the vigil. His place was eventually taken by Hans Bellert, who graduated from packhorses to a T-model Ford, until the line went out of commission, probably during the war. Now all that remain are a few cast iron posts and a swathe of clearing down Big Woody Island and along Fraser Island.

The Double Island Point lighthouse, perched at the top of the headland, was built fourteen years after its Sandy Cape neighbour. Its beam, magnified by optic lenses, flashes every 7.5 seconds and can be seen at Eurong on Fraser

Island and Noosa Heads on clear nights. Both Double Island Point and Sandy Cape are listed in the Register of the National Estate as light station groups, comprising light station, lightkeepers' cottages and ancillary buildings.

Because of the importance of the Great Sandy Strait to international shipping during the late nineteenth century, three manned light and semaphore stations were established, at Hook Point, Inskip Point and Big Woody Island. These three stations are now automated. Navigation lights were established at other points along the strait. A lightship was moored at the northern end of Breaksea Spit until removed in the 1970s.

*T*he 30-metre-tall Sandy Cape light tower was prefabricated in Bridgewater, England, and hauled by bullocks along the beach from Rooney Point.

THE COASTAL SANDMASS

*T*he high dunes of Fraser Island and Cooloola are scoured by the wind into magnificent sculptured masterpieces. These two giant sandmasses cover over 210 000 hectares, and the windblown sand rises from 65 metres below sea level to 250 metres above it. The rugged steep ridges, aligned in series by the prevailing south-easterly wind, run roughly parallel from the south-east to the north-west. The Great Sandy Region contains the world's most complete representation of sand dune systems extending back into the Pleistocene epoch (1.8 million years before the present).

During the Quaternary period (from 1.8 million years ago to the present), an enormous amount of sand was deposited around the coast of Australia. In the south and west of the continent these were calcareous sands, but along the eastern and northern coasts they were generally loose quartz sands. The greatest accumulations of quartz sands occurred in southern Queensland where sandmasses developed during several episodes of dune building. During the last four of these dune-building periods, at least, the dunes developed parabolic forms. This process is more developed in the Great Sandy Region than anywhere else in the world.

The sandmasses contain numerous examples of large parabolic dunes in various stages both of development and of degradation. On the exposed windward side, dunes are being shaped into sharper forms, while on the leeward side of the sandmasses weathering is eroding the dunes into a more subdued topography and leaching basic nutrients to a depth out of reach of

Above
A tree is engulfed by a slowly advancing wall of sand.

Left
*A*ncient coloured sands are cemented by small fractions of clay.

most plants. This results in very poor but very deep soils and a stunted vegetation. Chronosequences recorded in the Great Sandy Region are of international scientific importance because of the opportunities they provide to study the changes that have occurred with time, soil development and the biological systems which the soil supports — vegetation, soil invertebrates and fungal populations.

The region also contains more episodes of transgressive dunes than have been recorded anywhere else in the world. The parabolic dunes with lakes, the different kinds of active blowouts and their association with strand lines (old shore lines) present a unique array of geomorphological features. The combination of ancient beach ridge complexes and giant sandhills makes this region a unique coastal sand complex with the world's greatest sequence of Quaternary events in a non-glaciated area.

GEOLOGY

The region has two major geological elements: the high dunes of Fraser Island and the eastern part of Cooloola; and the sedimentary degraded sandstone areas of the upper Noosa River and Tin Can Bay. Outcrops of metamorphic rocks occur in the northern islands of the Great Sandy Strait, and igneous rocks outcrop at Indian Head and Waddy Point, and at Double Island Point.

The sandmasses are predominantly quartz sands. They contain less than 2 per cent of other minerals, mainly ilmenite, zircon and rutile with some feldspar. The quartz grains on the older surface beds are more weathered than their younger counterparts. The older sand beds may contain up to 15 per cent of silt and clay-sized particles in some zones. The sand sits atop predominantly sedimentary rocks, estimated to extend at least 30 metres below sea level. The thick, mainly unconsolidated sands contain layers of humate (peaty sand and sandrock bound by organic matter) and coloured sands. These are exposed in foreshore and cliff outcrops on sectors of the east coast recently cut back by marine erosion.

Sedimentary rocky outcrops occur on the tidal estuary of Boon Boon Creek, on Fraser Island, in an area visible only at low tide, on Big and Little Woody islands and the Duck and Picnic islands. All these outcrops are the result of upward folding of sedimentary bedrock of the Maryborough Basin. The bedrock is believed to be fossiliferous marine cherts of the Cretaceous period (135–65 million years before the present). In Cooloola the underlying rock is a Mesozoic (235–65 million years before the present) sandstone formation which strikes generally to the north-west and slopes from the Como Scarp beneath the Noosa River Basin.

Two pivotal hard rock areas are exposed in the sandmasses — Waddy Point and Indian Head on Fraser Island, and Double Island Point. These are thought to be tips of submarine volcanoes. Sand has accumulated around them, slowing down the weathering process of the rocks which were probably more massive and more extensive once.

The Waddy Point–Indian Head rocks are of Mesozoic or Tertiary (65–1.8 million years before the present) age. The rock itself, rhyolite, is a

*T*he northern end of Fraser Island has numerous lakes surrounded by low shrubby heath.

*M*ost of the loose windblown sand of the Great Sandy Region overlies
a mantle of coloured sands, vegetated by hardy dune species.

*I*ndian Head rocks are outcrops
of ancient volcanic rhyolite.

Facing page
*T*he loose windblown sand
derives its golden colouring from
a thin film of iron oxides coating
the normally milky white grains.

finely textured acidic rock characterised by its light natural colour, indicating
a high proportion of quartz. A little of the rhyolite of these outcrops was
used by Aborigines to make implements such as bowls but it was not used
for making knives and scrapers. The volcanic origin of Indian Head is
exemplified by the large-scale basaltic columnar jointing up to 10 metres high
on the north face.

The rocks of Double Island Point are also of volcanic origin but the rock
is andesite. The sand on the neck of land joining Double Island Point to the
sandmass is composed of calcarenite — calcareous sands cemented together by
calcium and magnesium carbonates. This differs from all other sands deposited
in the Great Sandy Region.

THE SAND AND ITS ORIGINS

The principal sources of nearshore sediment for coastal areas are the streams
and rivers that transport sand directly to the ocean. The sand is moved north
along the coast by wave action, wind and currents in a movement called
longshore transport. Some of this sand is moved onshore by wave action but
most of it is deposited as marine sediment just offshore. Eventually this
becomes the principal source of oceanic sands.

Sand is an aggregation of individual crystals which occur in roughly the
same proportion as in the constituent components of the parent rock. Since
silica constitutes the bulk of the parent rock material, silica grains make up

*C*oloured sands, caused when iron oxides have been leached downwards into another layer, are here exposed at the Cathedrals.

*T*hroughout the sandmasses of the Great Sandy Region there is a small
fraction of heavy mineral deposits of rutile and ilmenite, indicated by
black colouring in the sand.

almost all of quartz sand. The parent rock also contained very minor traces
of feldspars (a significant source of plant nutrients) and some heavy minerals
and this is reflected in the proportions in the sand. The size of the sand grains
varies considerably from 0.02 millimetre to 1.00 millimetre, with the most
common grain size around 0.2 millimetre.

Heavy mineral deposits are by no means evenly distributed throughout
the sandmass. They tend to be concentrated in lenses where the sand has been
worked and reworked by tides, and are thus found in greatest concentrations
along old shore lines. Because rutile and zircon are much heavier than the
silica sands, they are relatively easy to segregate from the sand, making them
keenly sought by miners. Plans to mine these heavy minerals first thrust
Cooloola and then Fraser Island into national prominence during the 1960s
and 1970s. Conservationists are pledged to preserve the natural vegetation,
ruggedness and beauty of these fragile areas, situated so close to the coastal
resorts where there is such great recreational demand.

The sandmasses contain both unconsolidated quartz, or oceanic, sands
and coloured sands. Coloured sands form the core of the sandmass but tend,
for the most part, to be buried and overlain by the more mobile oceanic sands.
Coloured sands are exposed only by erosion, mainly along the ocean beaches,
but can be found underlying the loose unconsolidated sands in most parts of
the sandmass. They are exposed along Rainbow beach and the Cathedrals.
Iron oxides have been released into the sands during their long history,
painting the sand with a rich variety of reds, browns, ochres and pastels.

*W*here the sand has been
worked and reworked by the
tides, even on ancient shorelines
some kilometres inland, mineral
sand occurs in thick black lenses.

*A*rtists have identified more than forty-seven colours in the spectacular coloured sands of Fraser Island and Cooloola. The unusual sculptures above occur near Cathedral Beach as sand and organic material combine.

*A*t Rainbow beach the sands have acquired an extraordinary sculptural quality.

Coloured sands are stickier and more cohesive than the oceanic sands because they contain a higher proportion of silts and clays which lightly bind the grains together. Because of these cementing agents the slopes of coloured sands can be much steeper than the oceanic sands, which have no cementing agents to hold them together.

The age of the coloured sands cannot be determined. They possibly date from before the Pleistocene epoch (more than 1.8 million years ago). It has been surmised that they have been immersed in the ocean and perhaps initiated as marine sand deposits. Because the coloured sands have been strongly modified by erosion, the initial shape and orientation of dunes are not evident, but they were once much higher and more extensive.

The oceanic sand is derived from two sources. Most comes from sand that has been carried along by the littoral transport systems, or directly from the ocean floor. The second but lesser source is from the leaching out of silt and clay and the reworking of the older underlying coloured sands.

Considerable research has been undertaken into the origin and development of the vast sandmasses. It has become increasingly apparent that while the origins of the sand can be explained, the build-up of the dunes is due to fluctuating sea levels. Quaternary fluctuations in sea levels periodically exposed large areas of sea bed. The force of intense onshore winds sweeping across these exposed oceanic plains piled the sand on the windward side of the existing dune systems to create new sequences of giant dunes. There have been several episodes of dune building.

*A*n alluvial fan at the base of the Rainbow beach cliffs is the result of erosion of the cliffs by the power of water.

*C*onsolidated sand is topped with stabilising vegetation.

*B*reaksea Spit is the northern extremity of the Great Sandy Region.

*P*atterns in the sand result from the tide and the crabs, one of the many species of animals that live beneath the surface of the Great Sandy Region.

During the four major glacial periods of the Pleistocene epoch, the icecaps of the poles slowly expanded and sea levels dropped, stranding the sandy plains of the ocean floor along the fringes of the great landmasses. Sea levels then were up to 100 metres lower than at present. During interglacial periods sea levels rose to approximately the present levels. The greatest interglacial period of 200 000 years occurred between the second and third glacial periods. High sea levels caused marine erosion of the dunes, resulting in a build-up of beach sands in the tidal zone. Falling sea levels mobilised this sand and caused it to be blown up on the windward side of the sandmass.

During the glacial periods winds of incredible velocity and strength whipped up the surface sediments and deposited them elsewhere. The coastal sandplains of eastern Australia, once covered by water, were swept by the winds that deposited the sand on the high dunes. This was the time of greatest dune building activity in the Great Sandy Region. A second major burst of dune building took place in the windy spells of the 'little ice ages' over the last 10 000 years. During these recent interglacial periods, the sea levels were high, and sand on the sea floor was delivered to the beach by the sea and carried inland by the wind.

As well as sea level changes, in places there has been a slow uplift of the land. This has saved some former beaches from subsequent wave attack, enabling scientists to unravel the mysteries of dunes and the sequences of their creation. Fossil remains of plants have been discovered in the layers of sand along the shoreline at Mudlo Rocks on Rainbow beach, 3 metres above the present beach. This is the highest Pleistocene shoreline yet recognised on the Queensland coast. Dating of the driftwood on this old beach established that the wood was over 40 000 years old.

Scientists have discovered that the process of building the dune systems of Fraser Island and Cooloola has occurred in a series of quite separate episodes many thousands of years apart. Except for the very oldest, all episodes can be distinguished, standing out from the air like growth rings in a tree or flood levels on a riverbank. The youngest systems are on the eastern side; the oldest dune systems occur on the western side of both sandmasses. There is a problem, though, in clarifying the age and identifying separate episodes in the very oldest dunes because the distinguishing characteristics of the dune systems are blurred and faded with time.

Soil scientists have established that the Cooloola dunes contain eight different systems, six of which appear to have remained exposed at the surface since they were first deposited. Scientists believe that the three youngest dune systems formed within the last 10 000 years after the most recent glaciation. The oldest systems extend back to at least the last interglacial period, which ended about 140 000 years ago. Some dunes may, in fact, be more than 400 000 years old.

Facing page
A sandblow marches across the landscape in a series of crescent-shaped waves but some melaleuca manage to keep their heads above the engulfing sand.

THE BEACHES AND DUNES

Beaches are constantly changing natural systems whose stability is determined by the amount and type of sand, the intensity of the natural forces and the stability of the sea level. Periods of erosion are normally balanced by periods of deposition. This balance is delicate and can easily be upset by a variation of energy, sediment supply or sea level.

Beaches recede when the capacity of the waves to transport sand exceeds the amount of new sand supplied by the system. High-energy storm waves erode sand from the beach. This sand is often deposited offshore as submerged sand bars. During periods of calm weather low-energy waves move sand from offshore sources and deposit it back on the beach to form a berm or sand ridge parallel to the shoreline. In several places the sea has eroded the older and higher dune deposits to form cliffs at the shore.

Dune building begins with the addition of sand to the beaches. As waves surge up to the beach they lose velocity and energy and thus they drop some of the sand suspended in the turbulent water on to the beach. During storms and cyclones, larger waves, which still have energy at the end of their run up the beach, drag more beach sand back into the surf zone than they carry up. At this time the level of the beach will be scoured down, sometimes even exposing extensive areas of 'coffee rock'. For most of the year, however, the winds are weaker and the waves are smaller. This allows the sea to restore the beach and build the dunes.

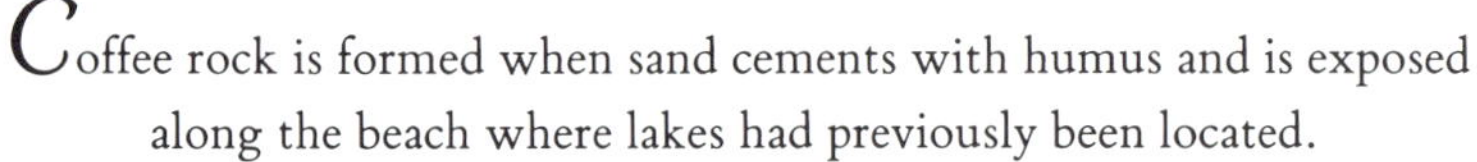

Coffee rock is formed when sand cements with humus and is exposed along the beach where lakes had previously been located.

*W*ind and rain together sculpt the sand of Fraser Island.

*W*athumba Creek is separated from Hervey Bay by a narrow isthmus of sand.

*H*ardy plants colonise the sandblows as they excavate down to the water
table, pioneering the way for a whole forest community to evolve over
time to heal naturally the scars of the blow.

Any wind with a velocity of more than 12 kilometres per hour will sweep the sand from even a wet beach towards the foredune. Onshore winds of sufficient velocity to move sand particles erode sand from the dry parts of the beach and transport it landward. In a process termed 'saltation', individual sand grains are carried by the wind close to the surface by a series of short hops. The wind sorts out the sand grains by size. Small particles tend to be removed from the beaches, leaving larger particles behind. The sand is trapped in the vegetation of the foredune, thus helping to increase the size of the dune itself.

Berms are formed on the upper part of the beach, outside the reach of normal high tides, by the wash of incoming waves. Waves shape the beach into a number of subtle ridges, bays and gutters. Cusps or ridges of sand running from the berm down to the water separate the beach into a series of mini-bays. Sometimes these bays are protected by a sandbar stretching out to cut off the surf and so establish a small gutter of quieter water. Fish are attracted to these gutters because the water is less turbulent and clearer so they can more easily see their food. Because the fish seek out the gutters, so do the fishermen. However, gutters do not remain in the same place for any extended period. The whole beach usually changes to some extent with the rising and falling of every tide.

Vegetation plays a dominant role in determining the size, shape and stability of dunes. The aerial parts of vegetation obstruct the wind and absorb its energy. Wind velocity near vegetation is thus reduced below that needed for sand transport and therefore the sand is deposited around the vegetation. Almost all the dunes rely on vegetation trapping the windblown sand to increase their size. Where vegetation fails to bind the sand sufficiently the dunes will be blown out.

Parallel dunes were formed as the sea level receded; they resulted from series of well-developed berms forming ridges parallel to the shore. Sand, trapped by debris and vegetation, increased the berm size. As the seas retreated a succession of new berms were created. The south-eastern part of Fraser Island represents an excellent example of this process.

Beach ridges are generally less than 10 metres above sea level and are largely restricted to parts of the coastline and sand islands where wave action is only moderate. They are therefore less liable to storm, wave and wind erosion. They tend to accumulate as the coastline advances, forming a series of low sandy ridges and swales which often contain lagoons or swampy areas. Moon Point, on Fraser Island, contains good examples of beach ridges.

Foredunes are built up at the back of beaches on the crests of berms and beach ridges where vegetation or other obstructions trap windblown sand. They become higher and wider as sand accretion continues. They act as barriers against the action of waves and tides, and are a source of sand for the beach during periods of erosion. They protect areas behind them from wave damage and tidal intrusion during storms.

Transgressive dunes have ridges aligned across the prevailing wind. These occur near Sandy Cape and south of Indian Head. Several sets of

*B*each spinifex (*Spinifex sericeus*) is a dominant sand-binding plant, helping to colonise the foredunes of the Great Sandy Region.

Sand driven north by littoral currents piles up on the southern side of Waddy Point and is then driven across the isthmus by the prevailing wind back into the littoral flow.

transgressive dune ridges are arranged roughly parallel to the ocean coast. Each ridge partly overlaps its predecessor and is stabilised beneath a cover of vegetation. Ridges range up to 60 metres in height and are of a relatively young age, possibly derived during the last interglacial period.

Blowouts or sandblows form when strong onshore winds erode a gap in a single foredune or series of beach ridges. The wind blows through the gap, sweeping sand from the beach and dune inland. Blowouts can also develop where the stabilising vegetation cover has been damaged or destroyed by natural causes such as droughts, fires and cyclones, or by human interference such as grazing, clearing or heavy pedestrian and vehicular traffic. If gaps in the dune system are not repaired, blowouts increase in size and migrate inland under the influence of the prevailing winds.

Parabolic dunes normally form in sandmasses carrying woodlands and forests. The vegetation on either side of the bare drifting sand traps some sand to create a characteristic shape. The term 'parabolic' was first used in Denmark in 1894, to describe blown-out dunes which had a 'U' or a 'V' shape. As blowouts are swept inland by prevailing winds, they develop an advancing nose of loose sand and trailing arms which have been partially fixed and stabilised by vegetation. Blowouts thus develop parabolic or 'U' shapes. The dunes retain a parabolic form as long as they remain partly vegetated so that the trailing arms are held back by vegetation. When the stabilising vegetation is removed the parabolic form is lost and wind action produces large transgressive sand dunes.

THE SANDBLOWS

Sandblows are large areas of bare sand where the sand is driven by the wind to form a horseshoe-shaped moving front. Sandblows have two sections. The largest is the windward side where the wind is excavating into the dune. In the leeward section the excavated sand is deposited, often engulfing any vegetation lying in the path.

Sandblows are mobile systems. While they begin in the fragile and vulnerable dunes, they are swept progressively inland until they are exhausted of energy or sand or have been overtaken by recolonising vegetation as a result of several consecutive good seasons. Initially they move rapidly. Some sandblows move many kilometres over hundreds or thousands of years. They may march at a rate of up to four metres a year, eroding foredunes particularly during windy years, but they tend to slow down once the sandblow has excavated down to the water table and vegetation cuts off much of the wind's energy. Observations indicate that the rate of advancement of major sandblows closed off from the strongest onshore winds such as that at Wabby Lakes and the Cooloola sand patch is between 40 and 90 centimetres per annum in normal years.

If the plants colonise the bare sand faster than the wind can expose new surfaces, gradually the vegetation may overtake or completely cover the sandblow. The vegetation creeps out both from the tongue in the centre and from the outside edges. Whether or not vegetation overtakes the sandblow

*P*atterns in the sand are left by the restless wind.

*L*ake Wabby is slowly being invaded by Hammerstone sandblow, which
acts as a barrage to help form the lake behind this wall of sand.

*K*nifeblade sandblow encroaches on trees that have already once been engulfed.

completely will depend on many factors, including the energy of the wind, the rainfall and the closeness of the water table. If the seasons are good and the water table remains high for long enough, vegetation may cover the sandblow completely. The slow progress of sandblows and the fact that they are swept uphill, defying gravitational pull, suggests that the term 'glaciers in reverse' is most appropriate. Like real glaciers, the sandblows leave behind powerful evidence of their progress in the form of the ridges that etch their former sides.

As sandblows move, they engulf and eventually bury the forests in front of them. As they advance further, they may exhume the remnants of the forests which they once interred. Some of these trees may have been entombed a thousand years earlier. However the sand-laden wind tends to blast into these desiccated wooden relics, causing rapid distintegration of their skeletal remains. Sandblows have become time capsules. As well as burying trees they have covered up significant Aboriginal cultural relics including stone artefacts. As the sandblows sweep forward they often uncover such relics, which remain unmoved by the wind as the sand below these heavier objects is swept away.

READING THE SAND

Soil develops on the sand dunes as the surface becomes stabilised. Dune soil types are known as *podzols*. The depth of soil development increases with the period of weathering (dune age) until it reaches a water table which alters the soil-forming processes. This ageing by weathering is indicated by the depth of the zone of white sand. In the deeper soils most of the nutrients are out of the reach of plants, thus stunting their growth and limiting the range of species. As the oldest dune systems are along the western flanks of the sandmasses, this is where the poorest and most stunted dune vegetation generally occurs. Although podzol soils occur widely throughout the world, the giant podzol soil profiles of Cooloola and Fraser Island, with depths over 25 metres, far exceed the known depths of podzol development anywhere else in the world.

Surface morphology is an excellent guide to the history of the dune sands in the Great Sandy Region. The periods of dune building can be readily distinguished and each is comparable in appearance, indicating evidence of periodic sand accumulation. The dune systems also reflect their ageing processes by their shape. On the east coast of the sandmasses the wind has its highest energy which results in the formation of sandblows. The steeper, more rugged dunes are usually the youngest. The least eroded dunes lie upwind of others with more degraded outlines. Evidence that younger dunes have invaded older, already vegetated ones, is common.

Sand is not a uniform even colour. Golden sand is normally observed on the beach, on the sandblows and in other places where the subsoil is freshly exposed. This colour fades with ageing. The golden sand gets its colour from a very fine proportion of feldspars and the fine film of iron oxide that envelops each silica grain. If the sand remains stable for a long time, the feldspars and

*T*he ancient, clay-impregnated, coloured sands that underly the sandmasses have been leached by age, wind and water.

*T*his skeleton of a once-great tree, buried and then exhumed by the
Kirrar sandblow, has been stripped of all its flesh by the furious blasts
of sand-laden wind.

Winds greater than 12 kilometres per hour will mobilise sand grains
even from the surface of wet sand and drive them along on an endless
cycle of burying and being themselves buried.

iron oxides become leached out and the sand fades to white. Pure silica sand is leached to a milky white colour. Where the topsoil has a grey colour this is due to the mixing of organic humus with the silica; this normally occurs only on the surface.

Subtle differences in the colour of the sand provide many other clues to the nutrient level. The more golden the colour is at the surface, the higher the nutrient level. Where the white sand extends to great depths, the nutrient level is low. This is reflected in sparser and more stunted trees. In the sandblows the topsoil is buried as the subsoil is heaped on top of it. However, the old soil profiles can be worked out by looking for the white and brown bands running across the path of the wind, which betray the shape and contour of the original topography.

Winds have the capacity to shape sandy beaches to form zeta curves in the shape of fish-hooks. The strength and direction of the wind determine the shape and orientation of the curves. In eastern Australia the prevailing south-easterly wind tends to align sandy beaches in a parallel, north-north-eastern orientation. The beach between Rooney Point and Moon Point is exposed only to northerly winds. This results in a different shaped zeta curve with a very different alignment.

On Fraser Island, the principal zeta curve terminates at Indian Head, while another starts at Waddy Point. Double Island Point is the link between two zeta curves, that of Wide Bay to the north and Laguna Bay to the south. The curves pivot from fixed rocky headlands such as Indian Head, Double Island Point and Noosa Head, which form the base or barb of the 'hook'. The beaches tend to run slightly obliquely to the angle of the prevailing wind hitting the coast. Zeta curves have common characteristics. At the base of the curve they usually have a sheltered bay with a series of sandbars and lagoons. This is exemplified by Wide Bay. At the terminal end of the beach sand accumulates either as a sand spit aligned with the wind (as it does at Inskip Point) or else heaped against the rocky headland.

On a calm sunny day, any person standing at the top of Double Island Point or Indian Head will see the sand seemingly suspended in an emulsion, being transported in the surf zone almost 180 degrees around the headland, at a rate of hundreds, if not thousands, of tonnes per day. Even this longshore transportation cannot fully keep up with all the sand drifting north along Teewah beach. Therefore, surplus sand accumulates and is trapped behind the headland. This is why the dunes in this part of Cooloola reach altitudes of more than 250 metres.

As well as the scientific importance of these geomorphic features, their variety adds to the region's scenic attractions. Vast areas of sand being swept by the wind, with the dynamics of death and life constantly struggling, provides a continuing source of fascination and inspiration. Here the natural processes occur so conspicuously. These wind-driven sand dunes are part of a complex cycle eroding and restructuring the sandmass. Watching the sandblows resculpturing the landscape is like witnessing the awesome action of mighty glaciers.

*T*he sand of the Great Sandy Region has been transported grain by grain through the surf zone from the rivers of New South Wales.

CLOTHING THE SAND

*I*t is not just the attractiveness of the Great Sandy Region's vegetation, but the great variety of plant communities, ranging from heathlands to the world's only luxuriant rainforest growing on high coastal dunes, which makes it exceptional. The whole region is covered by a patchwork quilt of vegetation types, and each landscape possesses its own unique collection of plants and communities. In some places there are trees over 50 metres in height and 3 metres in diameter; in others, small vines cling tenuously, with only a thin grasp on the loose sand. There are sharp delineations between these communities, with the change from treeless heaths to rainforests sometimes occurring in a matter of metres.

Patrick White perceptively described the vegetation of the Great Sandy Region in his novel, *A Fringe of Leaves*:

> Round them shimmered the light, the sand, and farther back, the darker, proprietary trees. Where the beach rose higher, to encroach on the forest, great mattresses of sand, far removed from the attention of the tides, were quilted and buttoned down by vines, a variety of convolvulus, its furled trumpets of a pale mauve. Vine-embroidered sand.

This description of 'vine-embroidered sand' perfectly illustrates how the loose sand is bound and stabilised by a cloak of vegetation. The wild and rugged terrain has been colonised and stabilised by tenacious plant communities.

*V*ines of angular pigface and beach spinifex embroider the sand.

*A*ncient melaleucas are the great survivors in the Great Sandy Region.

*O*ver 870 species of plants have been identified in the diverse habitats of the Great Sandy Region.

*E*verlasting daisies (*Helichrysum bracteatum*) grow prolifically along the foredunes of Fraser Island.

*P*ink pimelia is one of the many colourful wildflowers that grow in the heaths.

As one travels through Fraser Island and Cooloola, it is difficult to realise that this whole incredible biomass draws its mineral nourishment from the relatively inert sand, in which the small quantities of plant nutrients are concentrated. The minerals are derived from some of the grains of feldspars and the atmospheric fallout, subsequently recycled by countless generations of trees, and from minuscule amounts of aerosols delivered to the sandmass by the onshore winds.

Because of Fraser Island's size and the logistics of working there, its vegetation has not been as thoroughly documented and mapped as that of Cooloola, where botanists have identified 865 species of flowering plants and ferns in various plant communities, extending from sedgelands and wet heaths through various types of woodlands and grassy forests to closed sclerophyll forests and rainforests.

The Great Sandy Region is noted for its colourful wildflowers. At almost any time of the year, some plants will be putting on an attractive display. These annual short-lived bursts of flashing colour transform the land-scape, usually inconspicuous herbs cloaked only in khaki or dull green, into a spectacular and jumbled riot of colour. The rich variety of herbaceous flowering plants and some woody shrubs carry the most conspicuous blossom. The best array of wildflowers occurs on small herbs, orchids, lilies and other lowly plants.

*P*inkies (*Caladenia carnea*) are one of several ground orchids that thrive in the poor soils of the region.

*B*oronia rivularis (*above left*) is one of the more spectacular plants which are virtually endemic to the region. Angular pigface (*Carpobrotus glaucescens*) (*above centre*) plays an important part in binding the sand of the foredunes. As well as attracting insects, it is edible by humans. Wedding bush (*Ricinocarpos pinifolius*) (*above right*) is another common flower of the Great Sandy Region, while the distinctive berries of the chainfruit (*left*) can also be seen by the observant visitor.

*F*our flowers of the Great Sandy Region: pink wax flower (*Eriostemon australis*) (*top left*); beach primrose (*Oenothera drummondii*) (*top centre*); vanilla lily (*Sowerbaea juncea*) (*top right*); and pink iris (*Patersonia sericea*) (*above*).

THE FORMATION OF SOIL

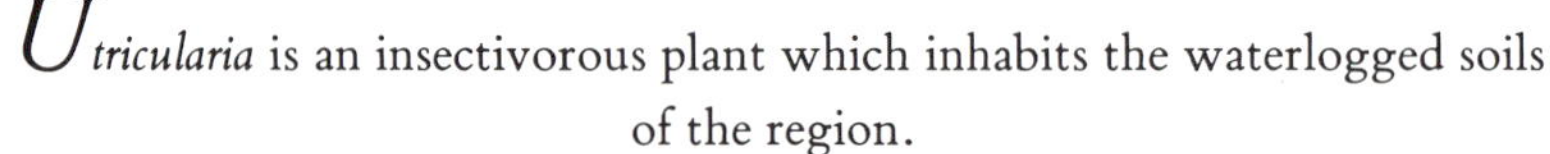

Bare sand contains small amounts of plant mineral nutrients. In raw sand nutrients are mostly associated with sesqui-oxides of the sand grains and with small amounts of feldspar. The sesqui-oxides and feldspars are the minerals responsible for the golden colour of the sand. Feldspars are derived from the parent rocks at the same time as the silica grains. Although feldspars are not as durable as silica, they retain minuscule amounts of potash and phosphates.

Ramifying through the sand beneath the dune vegetation are fine fungal threads called *hyphae*. Although hyphae abound, particularly in rainforests, even bare sand near the sea contains fungal spores. Hyphae grow from the roots of the plants colonising the youngest dunes. It is the presence of these fine hyphal threads that makes sand seem sticky, adhering to bare skin and polished material.

The associations between plant roots and fungal hyphae enable nutrients to be transferred by the hyphae from the sands to the plants. In return, the plants supply various organic compounds to the fungi. Because they lack chlorophyll, the hyphae cannot photosynthesise. They therefore depend on the plants for their nutrients. Once the means of exchanging nutrients between the sand and the plants has become established, soil is formed. The process of developing soils then proceeds very rapidly.

The soils of the sand dunes are mainly podzols, humus podzols and siliceous sands. The podzols are generally deep and freely drained, with a very low inherent fertility due to the siliceous parent materials. Because of differing

*R*osette sundews (*Drosera* sp.) thrive in the poor anaerobic soils by feeding on insects rather than photosynthesising their energy.

*U*tricularia is an insectivorous plant which inhabits the waterlogged soils of the region.

*T*he fruit of *Hakea gibbosa*, one of the common shrubs that grow on
better drained heaths of Cooloola.

rates of water erosion and sedimentation, soil development on the vegetated coastal dunes varies from site to site. However, the depth of soil increases with the period of weathering (dune age) until it reaches a water table which alters the soil-forming processes. A podzol age sequence has developed across the dune systems. Young dunes have a rudimentary profile, less than 50 centimetres thick; the oldest dunes have giant forms over 20 metres thick. The dune systems show that with age landforms due to water erosion become dominant and weathering eventually proceeds to great depths. Both Cooloola and Fraser Island contain giant podzol profiles with depths over 25 metres, which makes the soils the subject of enormous scientific interest.

THE NUTRIENT CYCLE

As soils develop and sands are vegetated, plant nutrients are transferred through the vegetation and organic matter on the developing soil surface. The nutrients are recycled almost as soon as any organic material comes into contact with the soil, where it quickly degrades to be taken up again. However, the nutrients held in the topsoil are weakly bound and easily leached.

Over the years, nutrients recycle many times over. They accumulate in some regions where the leaching has not been dramatic. In some cases nutrients may be relocated, by gradually migrating down the slopes to the valley floors. Associated with this process of changing nutrient status, certain plant species are overtaken and replaced by others which can better utilise the new conditions. As will be described, the plant succession can evolve towards a rainforest climax, or degrade down to heaths as the nutrient status changes.

Two former CSIRO scientists, Dr L.J. Webb and W.T. Williams, described the process of nutrient accumulation in an article in *Hemisphere* magazine in 1972:

> Nutrients from the sea-spray are blown by the wind on to the sand. As the droplets evaporate, the nutrients accumulate in a shallow layer on the surface. Spores or seed, blown by the wind or carried by birds, can now germinate, and a thin carpet of small plants develops. Once this happens, the minerals are secure, for as soon as a plant or a leaf or a rootlet dies, its nutrients are returned to the sand and picked up by the rootlets of neighbouring plants. So increasingly larger plants can be supported, all the time conserving the hard-won minerals.
>
> To use an ecological term, this constant recycling of nutrients constitutes a 'closed cycle': it can run indefinitely, unless some outside force intervenes to break the endless chain and so 'open up' the cycle. One such force is fire: if the community is burnt, the nutrients are released in the ash and may be leached by rain into hollows. Eventually the floors of deep valleys between the sand dunes are occupied by vine-forest species which are now protected from fire by the walls of sand around them. Thus the dune landscape and flats become mobile mosaic plant communities, all in different stages of recovery from the fires to which Australia is prone.

*B*are sand is quickly colonised by a rich variety of plants whenever the conditions permit.

Prevailing winds gather up a minute load of phosphates, potash and other essential elements during their long blast across the Pacific. They shed this in 'atmospheric fallout', which falls most heavily where it first comes in contact with land. To the west of the sandmass there is much less fallout than in areas closer to the sea, a consequence of which is that the height and density of vegetation in the western parts are much poorer.

In addition to the microscopic amounts of the basic minerals, plants also need another vital nutrient — nitrogen in the form of nitrates. This is obtained with the aid of specialised plants which have the capacity to convert atmospheric nitrogen to soluble nitrates with the aid of specialised bacteria attached to their roots. Such nitrogen-fixing plants then become the primary source of nitrates for other plants on the dunes. While most people know that plants in the legume family including wattles can produce nitrates, few appreciate that casuarinas also perform this function. Even ancient cycads, macrozamias, fix atmospheric nitrogen in the soil.

PLANT SUCCESSION

Plant succession is the process by which plant communities evolve. Normally plants move from pioneer species to reach a climax. Such succession from the early advance pioneers colonising bare sand to tall forests may take thousands of years. What makes the Great Sandy Region unique in the world is that plant succession works in two ways. In addition to gradually advancing (if conditions allow) towards rainforest, it also involves the degeneration of forest communities as the nutrients are leached out of the system.

Exposure to atmospheric salt markedly affects both plant succession and plant distribution. Only the most salt tolerant plants can survive the exposure in the heavy spray zones of the beach and foredunes. The beach grasses, creepers and beach oaks found on the foredunes are the most resistant plants to salt. The windswept form of coastal trees is the result of salt spray pruning. Further back from the beach are more salt sensitive plants, usually in the protection of dunes or other vegetation. Most forest trees are intolerant of salt on their foliage and thus develop best behind barrier dunes where they form a forest with a dense, aerodynamic leading edge.

In the Great Sandy Region there are two different processes of colonisation of sand — one where salt exposure is a factor and the other where it is not. Salt does not significantly affect colonisation of sandblows, but does affect the colonisation of bare sand near the coast. The creation of niches by different species begins on the foredune where there is a continuing struggle for survival against the salt-laden winds. The integrity of the frontal vegetation is essential to preserve the communities that grow in their lee.

Most of the foredune ground cover consists of vines, particularly fleshy vines or creepers such as angular pigface (*Carpobrotus glaucescens*) and goatsfoot convolvulus (*Ipomea pes-caprae*). Beach spinifex (*Spinifex sericeus*), scented fan flower and beach primrose all thrive in the salty conditions of the foredune. The plants of the sand dunes are not well adapted to drought. Their succu-

*G*oatsfoot convolvulus (*Ipomea pes-caprae*) is an important foredune ground cover.

*B*each spinifex (*Spinifex sericeus*) growing on the foredunes traps the sand swept from the beach by the wind.

*D*espite their tempting appearance, the fruits of the pandanus or screwpine have little nutritive value.

lence is not evidence of a dry climate, but the result of chloride accumulations in the plant tissue which causes the tissue to swell. These hardy and tenacious plants have thus developed a high tolerance to salt spray. They are frontiers where the vegetation of the sand dunes stretches out aggressively to establish new territory, and where the sea and the salt-laden wind retaliate with equal vigour to halt their advance. It is a struggle in which neither side wins. In the vanguard of the army of plants stretching towards the sea are both creepers and trees.

Beach spinifex and other creepers and grasses, including saltwater couch, sparsely bind the drifting sand to build up the foredunes. These grasses and creepers do not extend far from the foredunes, and are very susceptible to damage caused by use of the foredune for off-road vehicle access, camping or grazing. The delicate and fragile plant communities that bind the foredune together are subject to great pressure from feet, wheels and hooves. This is the pioneer vegetation most important to the stability of the sandmasses.

The trees offer a more permanent, more stable and more drought-resistant form of vegetation to consolidate the gains in sand accretion made primarily by the creepers. The trees and shrubs have graduated salt tolerances and one species seeks shelter from another. Invariably, the tree growing closest to the beach without any protection is the beach oak, sometimes called the horsetail oak (*Casuarina equisetifolia*) because of the shape of its foliage. Almost as far to the forefront are two forms of pandanus or screwpine (*Pandanus tectorius*) and coast banksias (*Banksia integrifolia*). In the lee of these are thickets of wild hops, wattles and other small shrubs, becoming denser as the protection from the wind develops. Behind these are coastal cypress (*Callitris columellaris*). In the lower, damper and more protected areas the paperbark (*Melaleuca quinquenervia*) occupies the niche.

Behind the cypress and paperbarks grow the eucalypts. Bloodwoods have the greatest tolerance to salt and wind. Pink bloodwood (*Eucalyptus intermedia*) and Moreton Bay ash (*E. tessellaris*) develop twisted, gnarled and tortured limbs that testify to their battles against the winds. Further back, the appropriately named scribbly gums (*E. signata*) and the smooth rusty gum or smooth-barked apple (*Angophora costata*) merge with them. In the most protected niches the giant blackbutts (*E. pilularis*) occur. These are characterised by their stringy-barked bases and bare gum bark tops, which have been eagerly sought by loggers. Grasses are displaced in the understorey by a great mixture of sedges including the delicate fluffy foxtail fern (*Caustis blakei*).

As well as the progressive plant succession described above, the region provides outstanding examples of both progressive and retrogressive forest succession. The stunted growth and the low woody heaths of the older dunes illustrate that the so-called climax forest is not self-sustaining. The status of the plant communities will deteriorate as soil fertility declines. Nowhere else in the world can this form of plant succession be so dramatically illustrated.

CSIRO studies at Cooloola have shown the strong relationship between vegetation type and depth of soil weathering. In these studies, the vegetation on different soils reflected the time gradient of forest succession. Soil and

*T*he adventitious roots of this ancient paperbark (*Melaleuca quinquenervia*) near Wabby Lakes bear testimony to how it has been engulfed in a sand blow and then had the sand swept away by the wind.

*E*verlasting daisies (*Helichrysum bracteatum*)
flourish on the foreshore.

*H*orsetail oaks (*Casuarina equisetifolia*) can survive where little else will grow.

vegetation data indicated progressive plant succession with increasing soil weathering on the younger dunes. On the older dunes, as weathering extends beyond the depth of rooting for many plants, retrogressive succession occurs. This illustrates the ultimate dependence of the communities on soil fertility. As nutrient reserves are depleted, or are leached out of reach of the plants, forests progressively deteriorate.

PLANT COMMUNITIES

The Great Sandy Region supports four main vegetation types, usually clearly separated from one another by narrow boundaries: rainforest, tall eucalypt sclerophyll forest, low sclerophyll forest with grassy woodland, and wet heath. In addition, there are at least six lesser communities, including melaleuca forests, cypress forests, tall dry heaths, coastal pioneer associations, riverine and estuarine fringe associations.

The rainforests (sometimes called 'vine scrubs') of the Great Sandy Region have received quite detailed attention from Dr L. J. Webb who identified them as a separate classification from other Australian rainforests. They are dominated by the satinay (*Syncarpia hillii*) and, to a lesser extent, brushbox (*Lophostemon confertus*) and characterised by such indicator species as the tall kauri pine (*Agathis robusta*), piccabeen palms (*Archontophoenix cunninghamiana*) and the smaller understorey species of carrol (*Backhousia myrtifolia*). Although both satinay and brushbox grow outside the rainforest, when they grow together with tall piccabeen palms and stately kauris with a carrol understorey, a rainforest community is established. This is usually associated with vines and epiphytes growing high in the trees, and with many other plants beneath striving for the light.

Other common trees of the rainforest are bumpy ash (*Flindersia schottiana*), crabapple (*Schizomeria ovata*), ribbonwood (*Euroschinus falcatus*) and bolly gum (*Litsea leefeana*). In the rainforest and wet gullies the piccabeen palms grow like gunbarrels, straight and leafless often for 25 metres. Strangler figs (*Ficus watkinsiana*) are among the most conspicuous and fascinating rainforest trees. Tree ferns are found in wetter gullies. As well as the vines of the Cissus family and Indian lawyer vine (*Flagellaria indica*) that drape from the canopy like tangled ribbons, staghorns (*Platycerium grande*), elkhorns (*P. bifurcatum*) and crowsnest ferns (*Asplenium australasicum*) are conspicuous epiphytes in this luxuriant environment. Orchids, particularly the brushbox orchid (*Dendrobium aemulum*), thrive in the rainforest.

About 6.5 per cent of Fraser Island (10 000 hectares) and 2542 hectares of Cooloola is covered with rainforest. The rainforests extend mainly down the central backbone of both sandmasses in well-protected sites, mainly interdune corridors. Some of the rainforest grows on sand dunes up to elevations of 260 metres. Very little of the rainforest of either sandmass has national park status. Only 809 hectares or about 30 per cent of Cooloola's rainforest is in the national park. While a slightly larger area of Fraser Island's rainforest is included in the Great Sandy National Park, it represents a much smaller percentage of the total rainforest area.

The tall forests of Fraser Island bear the scars of 130 years of logging.

*W*anggoolba Creek flows silently through Central Station under a rainforest canopy.

*I*mages from the rainforest: a king fern (*Angiopteris evecta*) at Central Station (*above*); lichens on a rainforest tree (*left*); and contrasting mature and juvenile leaves of a small-leaved lillypilly in Wanggoolba Creek (*below*).

Right

*L*ocal Aborigines knew this palm (*Archontophoenix cunninghamiana*) as *picci*. Today it is known as the piccabeen palm.

Leptospermum sp. growing in Cooloola National Park.

One of the many wattles (*Acacia* sp.) that flourish in the Great Sandy Region.

Fraser Island rainforest ranges from small isolated pockets to extensive stands irregularly distributed from near Hook Point at the south of the island as far north as Lake Bowarrady. Hoop pine (*Araucaria cunninghamiana*) occurs naturally in the northernmost rainforest pockets of Fraser Island, but only as far south as Eli Creek. Of Cooloola's rainforests Ramsays Scrub is the best developed and most complex. It is classified as complex notophyll vine forest. Other scrubs, namely Tramway, Broutha and Thannae, are described as either low microphyll vine forest or simple notophyll evergreen vine forest.

Rainforest also occurs on soils derived from shales and siltstone north of Kin Kin Creek. This is one of the last survivors of lowland vine forests on fertile soils in south-east Queensland. It is botanically distinct from the Great Sandy Region's sandmass rainforests, distinguished in part by the presence of proteaceous tree species, a family which is poorly represented in the rainforests of the sandmass. This small forest includes the notorious 'wait-a-while' lawyer cane which is not found in any other rainforest of the region.

The distinctive tall eucalypt forests dominated by pure stands of blackbutt (*Eucalyptus pilularis*) forest to mixtures of blackbutt with tallowwood (*E. microcorys*) occur mainly on the high dunes adjoining the rainforests at Cooloola and Fraser Island, and in a small area to the north of Kin Kin Creek. This zone, containing the main commercial hardwood, is to the lee of the first high dune and along the ridges surrounding the pockets of rainforest in the valleys. Here the most salt-sensitive trees are fully protected from the fury of the winds. This forest type also contains red bloodwood (*E. intermedia*), brushbox, some scribbly gum and forest oak (*Casuarina torulosa*). The dense understorey contains an even richer variety of species. This mix may vary considerably, depending on the topography and proximity of rainforest. The understorey frequently includes at the drier range species of geebung (*Persoonia*), *Acacia, Banksia* and *Leptospermum* and, in the wetter range, carrol (*Backhousia*).

Behind the foredunes, stretching back to the taller eucalypt forest, is a more open forest (low sclerophyll) dominated by colourful scribbly gums (*Eucalyptus signata*) with a lower canopy and grassy understorey. This community varies from one to three kilometres in width. It includes bloodwoods (*E. intermedia* and *E. tessellaris*), swamp box, smooth-barked apples, forest oaks and, in some lower areas, fan palms (*Livistonia australis*). A limited number of other eucalypts grow in protected pockets, including narrow-leafed ironbarks and forest red gums. Some distinctive understorey vegetation is encountered in this zone, including macrozamias, wattles and black she-oaks.

Open grassy woodlands and open forests also occur in the upper catchment of the Noosa River, the Wide Bay military training area, some of the islands of the Great Sandy Strait, and areas adjacent to Wathumba Creek on Fraser Island. *Banksia spinulosa* occurs only on the degraded sandstones and the western catchment of the upper Noosa River. This type of plant community was once widely represented in south-east Queensland. Due to the pressure of development, the once widespread *B. spinulosa* and scribbly gum communities are rapidly disappearing outside the Great Sandy Region.

*H*oop pine (*Araucaria cunninghamiana*) grows naturally in pockets of rainforest in the north of Fraser Island. This stand is part of a cultivated plantation on the island.

*T*he roots of a strangler fig begin to enmesh their host before fusing together to envelop it totally. Stranglers do not choke their hosts but rather overshadow and out-compete them.

Lichens, mosses and fungi thrive in the warm moist conditions of the rainforest where they play a significant role in breaking down fallen forest giants.

*C*abbage palms (*Livistona australis*) develop in association with the tall
sclerophyll forests, growing here at Hook Point.

A profusion of plants colonise the sand at Wathumba Creek.

Extensive treeless heaths are formed on the sand and peaty plains adjacent to the Noosa River, in some of the wetter dune swales, fringing many of the creeks on Fraser Island, and adjoining parts of the estuarine fringes. They are complex mixtures of shrubs (*Banksia robur* and *Leptospermum* species) and sedges. At their wet extreme the heaths grade into closed sedgelands where the giant sedge, swordgrass (*Gahnia sieberiana*), occurs, while the driest areas support mallee form eucalypts, low tree banksia and melaleucas. Some of Australia's more spectacular and colourful plant communities are found on the heathlands, and the Noosa plain is famous for its spring and summer wildflower displays.

Wedged between the foredunes and the tall forests as well as on the western fringes are some smaller forest pockets of distinctive types. Occupying the low-lying dunes in the sub-littoral zone is a forest dominated by cypress pine (*Callitris columellaris*). It grows on the better drained country. Paperbark (*Melaleuca quinquenervia*) grows in the lower lying and wetter areas. Paperbark forests occur on those areas of the drainage basin that have a seasonally high water table.

There is geomorphic evidence to indicate that some *Melaleuca quinquenervia* trees east of Lake Wabby are more than 2000 years old. These trees were probably in a wet area when engulfed by an advancing sandblow. They survived suffocation by metres of sand with the assistance of their adventitious roots. As the sandblow moved forward these advantitious roots were exhumed and still remain exposed as a testimony to their entombment

Swamp banksia (*Banksia robur*) growing at Boreen Point.

*M*angrove fruit, Hook Point, Fraser Island (*left*); and the delicate
flowers of a Cooloola mangrove (*right*).

*M*angroves and mistletoe at
Wathumba Creek. Mangroves
play an important role in the
region's ecosystem.

in the sand. Some melaleucas growing adjacent to Lake Wabby are buried
to a depth of more than 50 metres but they still survive. Because of this
survival capacity, melaleucas often appear to be growing out of place.

Shrubby woodlands to dwarf forests occur along the margins of the
sandmasses, particularly the western margins. Stunted mallee forests grow in
the north of Great Sandy National Park between the Sandy Cape lighthouse
and Ocean Lake. Few trees or shrubs are taller than one and a half metres.
In this dry heathland *Banksia oblongifolia* is the most prevalent banksia. This
type of forest does not occur elsewhere in the Great Sandy Region.

Mangroves represent the most significant and productive of Australia's
natural plant communities. They line the shores of Tin Can Bay Inlet, the
Great Sandy Strait and the Wathumba Creek estuary. They also occur along
the lower reaches of the Noosa River and Kin Kin Creek including Lake
Cootharaba. Of the twenty-nine species of mangroves in Australia, nine occur
in the Great Sandy Region. In addition, swamp she-oak (*Casuarina glauca*) has
been classified as a mangrove in this region because only here does it grow
in the intertidal zone.

There are also extensive seagrass beds in the Great Sandy Strait. More
than 12 500 hectares have so far been mapped. The outstanding features of
the seagrass communities are the dense and extensive meadows of 'dugong
grass' (*Cymodocea serrulata*) in the Great Sandy Strait. There are also dense
stands of eel grasses (*Zostera capricornia*, *Halodule univervis* and *Halophila ovalis*).

*M*angrove driftwood in Wathumba Creek.

*R*ed and grey mangroves in Wathumba Creek.

Low forest vegetates the banks of the Noosa River and Tewah Creek upstream from Fig Tree Lake. Common trees include cypress pine, swamp box and paperbark, while *Banksia robur* is a common low shrub of the riverbank vegetation. Occasional rainforest trees occur, with an isolated rainforest on the upper Noosa River, immediately adjacent to the treeless plain.

FORESTRY OPERATIONS

Although almost all of Fraser Island is vegetated, only 24 000 hectares (or 16 per cent of Fraser Island's total area) carries tall forests with commercial potential. This includes an estimated 12 000 hectares of blackbutt forest (8 per cent of the island), 7500 hectares of satinay–brush box (5 per cent) and 2400 hectares each of hoop pine rainforest and cypress forest (3 per cent). Virtually all the tallest forests occur south of Lake Bowarrady.

About 21 000 cubic metres of sawlogs are taken from Fraser Island annually in a logging operation which conservationists argue is having unacceptably adverse environmental impact. The subsidised logging operations of Fraser Island provide direct employment for fewer than 50 people. About 7480 hectares of Cooloola's forests are subject to logging. This includes some of the best blackbutt and rainforests outside the national park. The volume of timber extracted from Cooloola averages 2667 cubic metres annually. This is composed of about two-thirds hardwood, one-third scrub-woods, with only 150 cubic metres of kauri and hoop pines.

Studies have established that logging of both hardwood and rainforest timber in the Great Sandy Region has altered tree canopy cover over much of the area. Although there are few details of early logging of the Great Sandy Region's unique forests, it is known that most of the native kauri, hoop pines and white beech were virtually exterminated in the early period. Although there has been some regeneration of kauri, there has to date been little regeneration of white beech. Tallowwood and blackbutt have also been logged unsustainably. Prescribed burning to reduce the risk of wildfires in the logging areas has changed both the density and composition of the plant communities. Logging these forests and removing the timber is allowing the nutrient cycle to run down.

Forestry operations have also had a heavy impact on the natural environment through the construction of roads and the establishment of experimental plantings. Logging operations have resulted in the destruction of wilderness values, soil disturbance, a reduction in the average size of trees, manipulation of the fire regime, conflicts of values for logging and management access through national parks and the introduction and dissemination of plant diseases. *Phytophthora cinnamomi*, die-back disease, which kills some vegetation by destroying fine roots, has been introduced into the state forest areas. This disease tends to be transmitted in corridors along roadways, initially by vehicular movement.

The Queensland Forestry Department has ruled out the establishment of plantations of conifers within the Great Sandy Region, though there are

*O*ver a century of forestry operations has devastated the tall dune forests of Fraser Island and mainland Cooloola.

*S*atinay (*Syncarpia hillii*), the region's most conspicuous tree, takes 1000 years to reach maturity. It dominates the rainforest in which it grows.

*T*he buttressed roots of a blue quandong emerge from the leaf litter of the rainforest floor at Central Station.

a number of small residual experimental plantations. The productivity of the forest of Fraser Island is augmented by 'blackbutt enrichment'. The preservation of some virgin stands of timber within state forests relies on their declaration as 'Beauty Spots'. However the establishment of a 'Beauty Spot' confers no security of tenure as far as the long-term preservation of an area is concerned. Such 'reserves' are merely administrative decisions and have no formal legal status.

A UNIQUE ENVIRONMENT

The region's unique soils and vegetation patterns add to its other outstanding qualifications for World Heritage listing. It is the interaction of sand, vegetation and water which makes the Great Sandy Region unique.

The rainforests of these sandmasses are among the natural wonders of the world. Although other rainforests in the world (including several in Queensland and some beside the Amazon) grow on sand, the Great Sandy Region boasts the tallest rainforests growing on sand. It contains the only substantial examples of wet subtropical rainforest and wet evergreen vine forest with mixtures of conifers such as hoop pine and kauri pine in southeast Queensland. Many species reach the limits of their distribution in this important overlap zone. Rainforest species, including carrol and two species of mangroves, reach the southern limit of their distribution in the region.

While the rainforests of the sandmasses are outstanding, a more impressive feature to ecologists is the clearly demonstrable retrogressive plant succession that becomes evident as the soil fertility declines. Although podzols are the commonest soil types in the world, nowhere else in the world have such deep podzol soil profiles been measured. The soils of the sandmasses are amongst the deepest soils in the world.

The region's most conspicuous tree, satinay or peebang (*Syncarpia hillii*), and the vine *Tecomanthe hillii* are almost endemic to the area. Penda (*Xanthostemon oppositifolius*), a once common tree, now quite rare, is also virtually endemic. It also represents the major remaining habitat of the once common scribbly gum (*Eucalyptus signata*) and *Banksia spinulosa*. It contains several relict species such as *Argyrodendron trifoliolatum*, *Ficus watkinsiana*, *Gmelina leichhardtii*, *Melicope octandra*, *Planchonella australis*, *Dicksonia youngiae* and *Angiopteris evecta*. It also contains several endemic plants, including *Boronia rivularis*, *Boronia keysii*, *Marsdenia glandulifera*, *Drosera lovellae*, *Phebalium billardieri*, *Cinnamomum baileyanum* and *Grevillea hilliana*.

The prodigiousness of the biomass is demonstrated by the fact that when the volume was measured on one site of Fraser Island it was found that only one site in the world, the giant sequoia forests of California, had a greater measured biomass. The Great Sandy Region is a large area, ensuring that the integrity of most of the ecosystems can be maintained. The isolation of Fraser Island means that it is easier to protect its integrity from damaging invasions of exotic weeds and pests.

*P*hebalium woombye is a widely distributed shrub on Fraser Island, growing to 2 metres tall in the sandmass.

Left

*S*wamp ferns on Fraser Island.

Below

*R*eeds grow in the 'black' water of Lake Boomanjin.

Facing page

*S*edges in an unnamed swamp near Walameboulha Lagoon, Fraser Island.

A LAND OF LAKES

Almost as astonishing as the configuration of the sand dunes of the Great Sandy Region is the abundance of pure filtered water. It is all the more startling because it is so unexpected in such a porous medium that would normally have as much capacity to hold water as a tea strainer. The interaction of humus and sand provides features such as lakes, springs and streams. When sand mixes with organic material it rapidly develops a water-holding capacity. The sand may even become impervious to water if blended with enough humus.

Australia is a dry continent where lakes are relatively unusual and where most of the watercourses do not have permanent surface flows of water. The Australian mainland has no extensive lakes district, although the Central Plateau of Tasmania has a wealth of lakes and could be termed a lake district. Australia's second greatest concentration of lakes also occurs on an island — the largest island off the east coast, Fraser Island. There are forty named freshwater lakes in the region.

Aboriginal poet Oodgeroo Noonuccal (previously known as Kath Walker) referred to the damage to similar dune lakes on her home Stradbroke Island, in her poem 'Minjerriba'. She described Stradbroke Island as having 'Eyes brimming with waters so cool' before its exploitation by sandmining, and accused the exploiters of draining water from 'his ageless eyes'. The experience of Stradbroke Island inspired conservationists to fight to ensure that a similar fate does not befall the lakes of Fraser Island and Cooloola.

Above

Melaleuca roots at Lake Cootharaba, one of the region's tidal lakes.

Left

Basin Lake, Fraser Island, is one of the unique perched dune lakes.

'*B*lack' water flows across the beach from a stream on Fraser Island.

HYDROLOGY

The high annual rainfall exceeding 1500 millimetres has to go somewhere. A little rainwater runs off immediately and percolates through the porous sand to be added to the underground reservoirs. The sand soaks up the heavy rainfall like blotting paper and then slowly releases it at a constant rate. Sand has a lot of space between the grains which enables it when fully saturated to hold up to 30 per cent of its volume in water. The saturation does not extend all the way to the surface but is limited by the elevation of the regional water table.

The high dunes of the sandmasses act as an unconfined aquifer. The water from the aquifer flows across the beach sands in shallow streams, or emerges in springs from the beach, or flows through the beach below sea level. Many streams rise from springs in the water table. The water flow needed to sustain the streams and creeks is enormous, yet the volume in all streams flowing from the sandmass is relatively unaffected by seasonal fluctuations in rainfall.

The groundwater exists for the most part as a 'lens' in the sand, 'floating' over sea water. It extends up to 40 metres below sea level. The elevation of the regional water table lens rises the further it gets from the sea. The sand within the dune is relatively moist, even though the saturated sands are deeper down. The layer between the soil surface and the saturated zone acts as a vapour trap to prevent deeper drying. Some lakes and swamps in the interdunal low areas, or depressions, represent the upper level of the lens. Such lakes are simple window frames in the water table.

*T*his stream of 'white' water rises near Rainbow Gorge, runs for 100 metres and disappears.

Facing page

*T*he famous 'Bubbler' spring on Teewah beach.

The full potential of the freshwater resources of Fraser Island has yet to be fully assessed. Eli Creek is the largest creek flowing to Fraser Island's east with a volume of 80 million litres per day. Most of the island's larger streams flow west. These include Yankee Jack, Wanggoolba, Coongul, Woralie and Wathumba Creeks. Bogimbah Creek with a flow of 166 million litres per day is the largest flow yet measured on the island. These streams are potential future urban water supplies for mainland cities.

In some areas an accumulation of organic material has formed thick layers of peat. Water, gushing down the streams that rise in the sandmass, carves a meandering course through the peat beds, which confine the streams and make them narrower and deeper than they would otherwise be. Eli Creek for example, pouring forth a great volume of water, is contained in peat. It is deep and narrow where it is confined by the peat, but once it reaches the beach where it is unrestrained, it spreads out over a broad shallow course.

Most of the outflow from the Cooloola sandmass flows from springs. The northern part is drained by Searys Creek flowing into Tin Can Bay. On the eastern side the water flows through springs across the beach. To the west the water enters the Noosa River system either across the Noosa plain to the river or through its northernmost tributary, Tewah Creek.

In its lower reaches, the Noosa River is associated with a series of large shallow lakes through which it passes before reaching the Pacific Ocean just north of Noosa Heads. Kin Kin Creek drains land to the west of Cooloola into Lake Cootharaba near Kinaba Island. The sandstone of the Como escarpment acts as an aquifer, feeding the springs that run off east to join the Noosa River.

Movement of water on the Noosa plain and several treeless heaths on the western side of the sandmasses is influenced by the organic hardpan (humus podzols) at a shallow depth. The hardpan has formed on the top of the main aquifer, with a thin seasonal aquifer forming above it.

Many of the lakes occur at elevations many metres above the water table, which accounts for their description as 'perched lakes'. There are some very steep hydraulic gradients between a number of adjacent sites where the regional water table surfaces. This is an unusual feature which has not been recorded outside Australia. Even in Australia few perched lakes occur outside the Great Sandy Region.

Fraser Island has the highest perched dune lakes in the world (Boomerang Lakes — 130 metres above sea level) and the largest perched dune lake in the world (Lake Boomanjin with over 200 hectares of surface area). Most of the larger lakes are several metres deep. The water in the perched lakes is derived entirely from natural, heavy rainfall. Except for Lake Boomanjin, little run-off from surrounding catchments enters them.

The water is held in the groundwater table for a remarkably long time. CSIRO Division of Soils scientists tracked radioactive caesium, a by-product released during fallout from the atomic testing program at Maralinga in the 1950s. Much of the water takes several decades before emerging at springs.

Wathumba Creek on Fraser Island is a tidal estuary with a large freshwater catchment.

*L*ake Boomanjin, covering an area of over 200 hectares, is the largest
perched dune lake in the world.

*A*ncient melaleucas line most of the lakes. These sculptural roots are
at Lake Boomanjin.

The scientists estimated that the water moves laterally through the sand at
less than 66 centimetres per day, and that the water emerging from 'The
Bubbler', a spring on Teewah beach, had a mean residence period in the dunes
of about sixty years. Based on that observation, it is estimated that the mean
residence time of groundwater in the much larger Fraser Island sandmass
could exceed 100 years. Because some of the water may literally have come
down in the last shower, some of the water emerging from the dunes may
have fallen as rain more than 200 years ago.

BLACK AND WHITE WATER

Another source of wonder is the spectrum of colour of the water in the lakes
and streams. Colour ranges from a rich port wine red, through a variety of
tea shades, to pure and clear crystal. The darker, organic-stained water is
termed 'black water'. Its reddish to brown colour is due to organic material,
tannin from leaves and decaying vegetation staining the water in the same
way that tea-leaves stain tea — the more organic the additives, the stronger
the colour. Colourless water is termed 'white water'. Sometimes both types
of water occur in close proximity and may even merge in one stream. In one
example, the white water of Lake Birrabeen is joined by a narrow channel
to the stained 'black' water of Lake Jennings.

Although the volume and purity of the water in the creeks and lakes
of Fraser Island hold visitors in awe almost as much as the unique forests,

*T*he 'black' water of Lake
Boomanjin. The organic stains
of surface runoff have not been
removed by passing through the
filtering soil.

175

The sand lining the shores of Lake Birrabeen has been leached of iron oxides.

*L*ake McKenzie was created when organic material cemented the sand in a wind-formed depression.

few would be aware of the incredible processes that have created this phenomenon and fewer would be aware of the chemical qualities in the water which have excited scientists for decades.

Soil scientists investigating the water in the Great Sandy Region were mystified as to processes which accounted for white water and black water occurring so close together, especially as this is associated with the podzolisation processes. Elsewhere in the world white water is associated with lateritisation and black water with podzols but here that process was reversed. Eventually the scientists established that when black water flows through the soil the organic staining is removed by minute amounts of aluminium compounds present in the sesqui-oxides. The process is rather like throwing alum in a muddy pond or dam to settle out the clay colloids and make the water clear. As the sand filters through the dunes, the aluminium reacts with the electrically charged organic colloids, causing them to precipitate, leaving the water crystal clear. They concluded that all white water must have necessarily passed through the soil to clear off colouring colloids. All water in the regional water table as well as some water in the perched water lakes, such as Lake McKenzie and Lake Birrabeen, is 'white'.

The tranquil lakes of the Great Sandy Region contain very small quantities of nutrients. They are well oxygenated but of low biological productivity. They lack ions of calcium, phosphate and potash which make water

*L*ake McKenzie is one of forty perched dune lakes in the Great Sandy
Region. They are without parallel in Australia.

hard. The water is therefore extremely soft and very pure. Indeed, it is recognised chemically as some of the freshest natural water in the world. Mixing organic material with the water releases some organic acids causing water to become mildly acidic. Most lakes of the region have very dilute acidic waters.

Lakes with such interesting chemistry and construction are unusual in Australia — even in the world. They can easily become biologically degraded if human activities add nutrients, or substances such as detergents, to them. Inadvertent human usage may add phosphates, calcium and potash to the water. Even occasional use of soap, detergent or shampoo in or close to the lakes could change the character and biological balance in the chemical purity of the water. Urine would similarly affect the chemical quality of the water for centuries. Added chemicals will also reduce the freshness and softness of the water. Increased visitor use has placed stress on some of the more popular freshwater lakes through addition of bacteria. For example, *E. coli* counts of up to 46 parts per million have been measured in Lake Freshwater in Cooloola at times of heaviest usage.

THE DUNE LAKES

The mysterious lakes of Fraser Island and Cooloola have excited interest and comment for as long as people have observed them. Even before the turn of the century they attracted the attention of naturalists, writers and scientists. D. H. Lawrence referred to Fraser Island's dune lakes in his novel *Kangaroo*. He quoted a letter to the Sydney *Daily Telegraph* by Archibald Meston in 1905 which stated in part: 'The old Fraser Island Aborigines told me that a deep blue lake two miles from the White Cliffs, was once a level plateau, on which their fathers held corroborees, and that it sank in one night.'

Another early evocation came from Frank Dalby Davison in *Blue Coast Caravan*, in which he described them as having a 'sense of brooding even on a sunny afternoon. It was their darkness and stillness and their settings of bushclad hills untouched by the hand of man. It was an enduring mystery of the primitive that was felt — there was nothing sinister. They were natural curiosities . . .'

There are more than forty lakes in the Great Sandy Region. Most of them are relatively large, over 100 hectares in area. Most are more than 6 metres deep and many are over 100 metres in elevation, which seems remarkable considering the close proximity of the sea. Until 1978 most of these unusual lakes had not officially even been given names.

The lakes of the region can be divided into three kinds. Perched lakes occur in depressions where organic matter has accumulated to form imper-meable basements, or where impermeable layers of peat and sand come close to the surface. Window lakes are depressions where the land surface falls below the regional water table. Occasionally the water table brims over the surface to form window lakes or sparkling streams which gush through meandering peat beds in short dashes to the sea. Barrage lakes occur where

*L*ake Wabby was formed when a stream was dammed by a wall of moving sand.

*T*he numerous water table window lakes, such as this one in northern Fraser Island, continually surprise visitors who do not expect to find lakes in such a sandy environment.

*T*he sand spits in lakes such as Lake McKenzie indicate a great age. Spits
result from the currents established in the lake by the prevailing wind.
The lunette dunes on the lakes are of great scientific interest in indicating
major climatic changes.

*L*ake Poona is one of the region's perched dune lakes. Here, the system
has no outlet and pollutants put in the lake may not be removed for
hundreds of years.

watercourses are obstructed by mobile sand dunes. Interestingly, seismic
scientists have now begun to investigate if Yankee Jack Lake was the lake
referred to by Meston. They may establish a new category of dune lake for
Fraser Island.

Although lakes occur in dunes in many areas of the world, the Australian perched lakes situated in high, leached, siliceous dunes appear to be
unique. Their mode of origin, through a combination of wind action and
organic accumulation, may be peculiar to eastern Australia. At least such
occurrences are rare elsewhere. It was only during the 1960s that scientists
were able to identify the nature of these lakes. The perched dune lakes include
the well-known Lakes McKenzie, Poona, Boomanjin and Birrabeen.

The depressions in which the lakes are formed are caused by advancing
walls of sand being swept along by the wind sealing off a valley and then
being stabilised by overtaking vegetation before the valley is completely filled.
However, because of the porosity of the sand, this alone is not sufficient to
form a lake. Instead, the depression accumulates leaf mould and organic
detritus which cements the sand into an impervious seal. Once that organic
seal is in place, the depression will hold water and lakes begin to form. The
resulting development is an attractive interaction of water, sand and tall
forests. The lake sediments consist of detritus or organic silt. This chalky-
textured humate enables many lakes to be elevated well above the water table.

*L*ake Poona, Cooloola.

A series of radiocarbon datings carried out by scientists at Hidden Lake suggests that the organic deposits in the lakes date back to at least about 10 000 years before the present.

Several lakes are more than 100 metres above sea level with startlingly steep hydraulic gradients which could amount to subterranean waterfalls if they were connected with the regional water table. Because the lakes are obviously not connected but well above the water table, they are called 'perched dune lakes'. Scientists have studied Hidden Lake, which is typical of many perched lakes. They drilled around the lake just 50 metres from the water's edge, but encountered no water at or well below the level of the lake's surface. This research established two things. It proved firstly that the lake was perched; and secondly that its catchment was virtually restricted only to the rain that fell on the lake's surface. It caught almost no run-off.

Because of the lack of run-off, water levels in the perched lakes can fluctuate quite dramatically. In 1973, for example, after three very wet years, water in Lake McKenzie was exceptionally high. It was up in the vegetation about 3 to 4 metres or more than the mean lake levels a decade or so later. There was absolutely none of the magnificent white beach visible at all. However, the water in Ocean Lake would not have risen or fallen more than a metre in this period. The lakes that vary most in levels according to the rainfall are most likely to be perched lakes. Ocean Lake, whose level remains relatively constant, is typical of the window lakes.

Only the perched dune lakes seem to have well-developed beaches. These are almost always on the north-western shores, which have been exposed to the lapping of the waves driven by the omnipresent south-easterly winds. These beaches of pearly white sand, leached of the film of iron oxides, enhance the aesthetic appeal of the lakes. The same wave action that establishes the beaches also tends to establish sand spits as a result of internal currents created by the wind. After some eons these spits can develop to the point of segmenting some of the oldest lakes such as Lake Benaroon.

Remarkable features of many of the lakes are the dunes or lunettes on the leeward sides which are being further sculptured by the winds. It is in such lunettes that many of the archeological finds at Lake Mungo in western New South Wales have been found. These are a symptom of the great age of the lakes. The older perched lakes tend to develop foredunes and even sandblows in these dune systems, such as one finds at Lake Boomanjin. These wind-induced features and lakeside beach ridges are rare and require further detailed study to discover new information on lake hydrology.

Wabby Lakes are not perched in the same way as most of the other Fraser Island lakes. They are formed by a wall of sand being swept across a small stream to dam it, thus forming two beautiful lakes behind it. Technically known as barrage dune lakes, Wabby Lakes are the least acid of Fraser Island's lakes. At 11.4 metres Big Lake Wabby is the island's deepest lake. It supports more than seven species of fish and a greater variety of birds than the other lakes. Wabby comes from the Aboriginal *Wahba* meaning 'place of crows'.

Reflections in the Noosa River.

ACID WATER WILDLIFE

Because of their filtered purity, high acidity and low levels of chemical nutrients, the lakes are not very productive habitats for fish and other aquatic fauna. Only a few specialised fish species and other aquatic organisms can tolerate this environment.

Most of the lakes support only three species of small fish, although most contain turtles. With so little prey there are few waterbirds to be seen around the lakes. One scientist spent a number of years studying the freshwater turtles in Lake Coomboo. He was astonished that he was able to identify more than 800 individual turtles in a lake that had very few nutrients and food sources in its 15 hectares.

Small numbers of musk ducks here reach the most northerly part of the Australian range, and a few little grebes may be found in the lakes, but there are few if any other waterbirds. The lakes with the greatest abundance of bird and fish life are the two Wabby Lakes. Some sizeable fish, such as Australian bass and flagtail perch, shelter in the reeds and in the shelter of snags and underwater overhangs of the peat banks of the freshwater streams. The most unique fauna of these very acidic aquatic conditions are the 'acid frogs' which can tolerate the acidic conditions of the lakes and the organic swamps.

A freshwater turtle (*Emydura kreftii*). The pure, filtered water of the lakes does not sustain much aquatic life other than a few species of fish and amphibia such as a group of 'acid frogs' adapted to the acidic conditions.

BEACH HUMATE ROCKS

As one travels along the region's expansive beaches one encounters occasional outcrops of what appear to be rocks on the beach. In fact, these black rocky-looking boulders are not true rocks. Rather, they are the remnants of old lake or creek beds. The material is no more than humus-impregnated sand — humate. It is variously called indurated sand and coffee rock but the name 'humate' is more appropriate, because it gives a clue to the origin of the 'rock', sand cemented with humous material. Although resistant to the sea, the humate is not really hard. It can be broken off by hand, crumbled up with an axe and worn away by solid friction.

As the sea erodes away the dunes it often exposes the beds of old lakes, swamps or creeks. The humate is more durable than the looser unconsolidated oceanic sand and resists the sea more steadfastly. When the beach is badly eroded, the humate rocks form difficult obstacles for beach traffic. At times of great beach erosion, beach levels may lose up to 4 metres of sand, exposing new fields of rocks which are normally buried in the beach.

THE NOOSA RIVER

The Noosa River is the very heart of Cooloola. This silent, serene and secretive waterway feels its meandering way from the Como Scarp through the expansive treeless plain before it meets Tewah Creek to form a 65-kilometre stretch of navigable waterway. It barely moves through the long avenues of melaleucas fringing the banks of its middle reaches. It disappears into the shallow Lakes of Figtree, little more than knee-deep, and moves

*T*he meandering Noosa River in the heart of Cooloola reflects the
forests that line its peaceful banks.

*I*n its upper reaches the Noosa River carves its way through the Noosa Plain.

*G*narled melaleuca roots on the edge of Lake Cootharaba.

through Cootharaba and Cooroibah, past Tewantin, where Lake Doonella is an offshoot, and past Noosaville to reach the sea in Laguna Bay.

When sea levels were much higher and Cooloola was an island, the Noosa River was linked to Tin Can Bay, extending Great Sandy Strait to Noosa Heads. The headwaters of Tewah Creek are no more than 8 metres above Tin Can Bay. The watershed is adjacent to the sandstone mass Mt Bilewilam (93 metres) on the western side of the sandmass. The sluggish Noosa River takes more than 60 kilometres to fall these few metres.

Kathleen McArthur, a conservationist who pioneered the cause for Cooloola's protection, vividly described Tewah Creek in her book *A Living River — the Noosa*:

Tewah, the young and slim, is seen to slip sinuously, curvaceously and colourfully trailing swirls of deep red dye, leached from the peat beds, around trees fallen especially to provide sun-baking water dragons with a midday siesta. When Tewah joins mother river she loses her identity completely.

She went on to describe the Noosa River:

Never in a hurry, even in floodtime when the surplus water gently and silently spreads over the surrounding low-lying land, the deep straight-banked river moves slowly down, gathering reflections of bare armed Scribbly Gums beside black bodied Aboriginal Coolooli and the dark haired Casuarinas and cork berries that entice Top Knot Pigeons down from the rainforests when their black fruit is ripe and Banksias, peopled with weird, hairy-men and Bloodwoods snowcovered with blossom in mid-summer and twisted paperbarks dipping fingers in the water to animate their reflected stark white trunks with ripples. Between the river trees and their reflections are the reed-covered shallows and fern held banks spotted with sundews where crimson Boronia grows with white weeping Tea-tree, yellow Bush Peas, pink Nunyi-um, Blueberry Ash, and Blackboys which 'stood so still so many a year they grew leaves in place of hair'. Binding all together in this kaleidoscopic ribbon is the colour and the pattern of the sky above.

In its middle reaches, before flowing through the tidal lakes, the Noosa River is 3 to 5 metres deep and averages 30 metres in width. It is one of the best remaining streams for fishing for Australian bass (*Macquaria novemaculeata*). Although it descends to the salt water each year to breed, this fish requires unpolluted clear streams to survive and flourish. Although navigable for several kilometres, the most charming section is between Harry's Hut and the lakes in a section called 'the narrows' where the melaleucas reach out almost to touch river-borne explorers and the tannin-stained water reflects the dense vegetation. Harry's Hut is an excellent camping and picnic spot.

Facing page

*I*n its lower middle reaches, popularly known as the 'Everglades', the Noosa River is lined by large rafts of sedges.

*U*nder these trees at Elanda Point, Aborigines held their corroborees
until about 1860 when their lifestyle of 40 000 years was shattered.

RIVER LAKES

No other river system in Queensland is endowed with such a large expanse of lakes. The Noosa River has five tidal lakes: Como, Cooroibah, Doonella, Weyba and Cootharaba. Lake Cooloola, a very acidic freshwater lake, may once have been part of the river system but it is now isolated and is only flushed out and recharged during flood. As the water remains unchanged it accumulates increasing concentrations of humic acids until the next flood rains occur.

Lake Como is fed by two freshwater streams making its water almost drinkable. Its shallow depth does not diminish its value as a waterfowl habitat. The two largest lakes, Cootharaba and Cooroibah, straddle the Noosa River. Lake Cootharaba, the largest of all, covers thousands of hectares but is no more than 2.5 metres deep. Boreen and Elanda Points on the shores of this sheltered, shallow lake are very popular with sailing enthusiasts.

These river lakes are subject to tidal influence but the range at Lake Cootharaba is less than 30 centimetres and tides occur only twice a month, at full moon and new moon. The shallow brackish water attracts large flocks of waterbirds, particularly pelicans. Lake Cootharaba's extensive beds of eel grass (*Zostera*) consist of submerged vegetation which thrives in the warm shallow waters of the lake, making it an ideal habitat for prawns.

Nowhere is the heritage of the Great Sandy Region more precious nor more vulnerable than in the fresh and pure water of its lakes. The lakes must be cherished, protected and passed on to future generations, with the same pristine beauty they now have. The very minimum bequest which this generation can endow is to ensure that all the lakes and their environs are given the national park status which pioneering scientists first advocated a century ago. Only then will they be secure.

*L*ake Cootharaba is the largest of the tidal lakes on the Noosa River, but the tidal variation is almost imperceptible and occurs only twice monthly.

FISH, FOWL AND OTHER FAUNA

The vast biomass of vegetation in the Great Sandy Region is not matched by an equivalent density of fauna. However, it is not the quantity but the diversity and rarity of the fauna which make it particularly interesting. The region has an exceptionally high diversity and population of birds. The marine fauna is both prolific and diverse, ranging from whales to whiting and from dugong to shrimps. Sand swimmers such as earthworms and sand crawlers, particularly insects that can take advantage of the loose sand, thrive. Although the Great Sandy Region lacks large populations of bigger terrestrial animals, the small numbers are more than offset by the variety of rare species.

The region is an overlap area. Several species reach their northern limit and coincidentally many other species reach their most southern range here. As a result there are particular associations of fauna that occur nowhere else.

MAMMALS

The paucity of mammal species is due, in part, to the fact that the vegetation is low in grasses and other sources of edible and digestible proteins. However, the region is a significant habitat of a number of uncommon mammal species. For example, the false water rat (*Xeromys myoides*) almost reaches the southernmost part of its range here. The attractive yellow-bellied (or fluffy) glider (*Petaurus australis*) has the unusual habit of cultivating its territory to harvest the saps of particular eucalypts.

Above
A brahminy kite soars above Fraser Island.

Left
Hervey Bay, Tin Can Bay and the Great Sandy Strait are significant dugong habitats.

The most prodigious species of mammals are bats, particularly the flying foxes. Large colonies of flying foxes, including grey-headed fruit bats (*Pteropus poliocephalus*), live in the rainforest and mangroves, and feed on the blossoms and fruits of the melaleucas and other trees. A number of other bats, among them the lesser long-eared bat (*Nyctophilus geoffroyi*) and light-bellied shear-tailed bat (*Taphozous flaviventris*), live in the hollows of the larger trees. Queensland blossom bats (*Synconycteris australis*), smaller than many species of butterflies, flourish on the blossom of the banksias with the same relish as past generations of Aborigines. They are rarely seen because of their diminutive size and nocturnal habits.

Arboreal mammals are uncommon. There are a few other species of gliders as well as possums but nowhere are they numerous. There are no longer any koalas on Fraser Island, although it does have an abundance of favourable trees. Rollo Petrie recalls learning about koalas being on Fraser Island as a boy in 1911:

> Old blacks, Teddy Brown and Nugget, told us why there were no koalas on Fraser Island. There was a really long Aboriginal story about an old man bear, the last of his tribe; the others had died or been eaten. He used to live up in a very big gum tree and down near Fig Tree Creek — it was right on the coast. This last big bear lived up that tree and he'd come down at night and he'd cry at the foot of the tree, sit there and put his hands over his eyes and cry (the Koala can cry like a baby) but he'd go back up when daylight came, sit up in his branch all day. This went on for years and years until he became sacred to the blacks. They wouldn't eat him, they wouldn't kill him. (He was probably too tough, anyhow.) He eventually died with his hands over his eyes at the foot of the tree and that tree was more or less sacred because he was the last koala on the island. The bears had been a source of food.

*T*he purest strain of dingo in eastern Australia is found on Fraser Island.

It is possible that Aboriginal hunting pressure also exterminated both scrub turkeys and emus on Fraser Island. Although common on Cooloola, they do not occur on the island.

Except for the swamp wallaby (*Wallabia bicolor*), which is not prolific, there are few macropods. There are a few Eastern grey kangaroos (*Macropus giganteus*), mainly in the Womalah landscape, but they are rare in the sandmass. Most of those observed on western Fraser Island are only casual visitors which swim across Great Sandy Strait.

The mammals that flourish best are those that rely on digging, such as echidnas, bandicoots and native rodents. These include the Australian water rat (*Hydromys chrysogaster*), fawn-footed melomys (*Melomys cervinipes*), grassland melomys (*Melomys burtoni*), little native mouse (*Pseudomys delicatulus*), southern bush rat (*Rattus fuscipes*), eastern swamp rat (*Rattus lutreolus*) and the pale field rat (*Rattus tunneyi*). The occasional platypus can be seen by the patient observer as it plays and feeds in the tea-coloured waters of the upper Noosa River.

*T*he fawn-footed melomys (*Melomys cervinipes*) is a common mammal.

The dingo (*Canis familiaris*) population of Fraser Island, of between two and three hundred, is regarded as the purest strain remaining in eastern Australia. Domestic dogs pose a threat to the dingoes by hybridisation and, more ominously, by transmitting canine diseases such as *Parvo* virus to them. Horses were introduced to Fraser Island in the 1870s and provided a parent stock for the present feral horses (brumbies). Brumbies are also found in western Cooloola, although populations are now declining in the region.

Big Woody Island was once overrun by feral animals, including goats and rabbits. There are still some goats there but Woody Island is the only known place in the world where a rabbit colony has been completely exterminated by the myxomatosis virus. A few feral cats and cattle may survive on Fraser Island but they are very elusive. In Cooloola introduced fauna pests include the hare (*Lepus europaeus*) and the fox (*Vulpes vulpes*).

BIRDS

The Great Sandy Region has a remarkable diversity of birds — more than 230 species have been recorded in the region. This prolific birdlife is a major attraction for both Australian and overseas visitors.

The last remaining populations of coastal emus in Queensland are found in Cooloola, characterised by a darker plumage than their inland counterparts. They enjoy a sweet life in Cooloola and a lucky observer may catch the unusual sight of a group of emus taking a swim in one of the lakes.

Among the more unusual birds of the region is the southern emu wren (*Stipiturus malachurus*), which has so far been recorded in Queensland only

*P*elicans like the quiet waters of the rivers and estuaries of the Great Sandy Region.

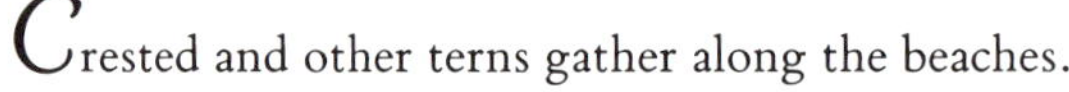

*C*rested and other terns gather along the beaches.

Sharing a beach with only a dingo is a rare privilege in a world where wilderness is becoming increasingly rare.

*T*he blue-faced honeyeater (*Entomyzon cyanotis*) is but one of the birds
of this region, which boasts a great diversity of species.

*R*ainbow lorikeets (*Trichoglossus
haematodus*) occur in huge flocks
to feed on nectar and at many
bird feeders in the nearby city
of Hervey Bay.

from the Noosa plain. The turquoise parrot (*Neophema pulchella*), normally associated with the drier inland areas, was also recorded at Cooloola. The glossy black cockatoo (*Calyptorhynchus lathami*), which is common in Cooloola, has a very limited distribution outside the region. One of the rarest Australian birds, the ground parrot (*Pezoporus wallicus*), whose very specific habitat elsewhere in eastern Australia is rapidly disappearing, is relatively common in the heathlands of the region where its populations are stable. The Great Sandy Region contains a number of other rare and uncommon species including the brush bronze pigeon (*Phaps elegans*), powerful owl (*Ninox strenua*), grass owl (*Tyto longimembris*), plumed frogmouth (*Podargus ocellatus plumiferus*) and peregrine falcon (*Falco peregrinus*).

The wading birds are an interesting feature of the region. Tin Can Bay and Great Sandy Strait are important stopovers on the flyways for trans-equatorial migratory wading birds flying between southern Australia and their breeding grounds in Siberia for the northern summer. Two different flyways converge on the strait, making it a vital area for migratory birds. Each autumn these birds fly north to Siberia, where they briefly exchange their almost uniform drab brown colours that we associate with them in Australia for brighter breeding plumage. Before they begin their long flight back to Australia they have shed most of their technicolour feathers in favour of their dreary garb again. They return south from late September and early November. Huge populations of waders rest for some days in the Great Sandy Strait during the trans-equatorial migrations.

*C*rested pigeons (*Ocyphaps lophotes*) are attracted to open grassy areas of
the Great Sandy Region.

*T*he red-capped dotterel (*Charadrius ruficapillus*) is a year-round resident,
common along the ocean beaches.

With over 14 per cent of the population, the Great Sandy Strait is the most important Australian habitat for the eastern curlew (*Numenius madagascariensis*). It is among the four most important Australian sites for bar-tailed godwits (*Limosa lapponica*) and Mongolian sand-plovers (*Charadrius mongolus*). Great Sandy Strait is also a very significant habitat for many immature waders that remain in the region during the Australian winter. Because of the international significance of migratory waders and evidence of the Great Sandy Strait's pre-eminence as a wader habitat, a continuing wader research project into their distribution and abundance is being conducted. This is part of Australia's contribution to a co-operative project which includes Japan, China, Alaska, South Korea and New Zealand.

REPTILES AND AMPHIBIA

Twenty-three amphibians and forty-six terrestrial reptiles have been recorded in the Great Sandy Region. The unusually acid water of the swamps and lakes has given rise to 'acid frogs' confined to the wallum areas of Queensland and New South Wales. Among them are the wallum rocket frog (*Litoria freycineti*), Cooloola tree frog (*L. cooloolensis*), white striped tree frog (*L. olongburensis*) and wallum froglet (*Ranidella tinnula*). The acid frogs depend upon the availability of acid water to facilitate the development of their larvae. Although the high acidity excludes non-acid species (of which there are nine in the region) from the habitat, it also restricts the distribution of the acid frogs to the wallum wetlands. In areas disturbed by roads, buildings or forestry activities, non-acid species of frogs are able to invade the habitat of the acid frogs.

*G*reat Sandy Strait is an important habitat for the eastern curlew (*Numenius madagascariensis*).

*P*eron's tree frog (*Litoria peronii*). The Great Sandy Region provides most of the world's habitat for acid frogs.

There are also some unusual records of reptiles. For example, one of the few reportings of the four-fingered skink comes from Cooloola. Although there are also other venomous species of snakes, including taipans, death adders and brown snakes, they are rarely seen unless they are sought. One previously undescribed species of blind snake (*Ramphotyphlops*) is restricted to the heathlands of Cooloola. The tiger snake (*Notechis scutatis*) reaches its northern limit in the region. The three-toed reduced limb skink (*Anolopus* cf. *aphioscincus*) is a recently discovered species which is believed to be endemic to the rainforests of the region.

Cane toads (*Bufo marinus*) are extremely common within the Great Sandy Region. These introduced pests occupy niches of native species, and until the indigenous fauna developed means of coexisting with them, the cane toads had a devastating effect. Now, many bird species, including cattle egrets, eat immature toads before their glands develop the infamous lethal properties. Other birds, including crows and kookaburras, have learnt to attack adult toads, turn them on their backs and remove only the viscera, thus avoiding the poison in the back of the toads. As a result of these predations, populations of cane toads in the region have contracted.

*C*ane toads (*Bufo marinus*) are introduced pests which have invaded the Great Sandy Region and now threaten native frogs.

*T*he carpet python, a sand basker, is one of eleven species of land snakes recorded from the Great Sandy Region.

*G*oannas or sand monitors are conspicuous scavengers near picnic spots.

*K*reft's river turtle (*Emydura kreftii*) occurs in large numbers in the perched lakes of the Great Sandy Region. More than 800 have been located in Lake Coomboo.

FRESHWATER FAUNA

Although the freshwater lakes and streams are unable to maintain large aggregations of waterfowl, they have some interesting fish. The isolation of the lakes, both from the ocean and from each other, has enabled each lake to develop its own distinctive fauna. Some of the fish, including small rainbow fish (*Rhadinocentrus ornatus* and *Hypseleotris klunzingeri*), have presumably been introduced as eggs on the feet of birds. A new species of sunfish (*Melanotaenia* sp. nov.) was recently found in Lake Boomanjin, Lake Wabby and Red Lagoon of Fraser Island. It had previously not been recorded as far south. The lakes appear to be free of the cannibalistic introduced mosquito fish (*Gambusia affinis*) which seem to have affected the distribution of the rainbow fish elsewhere in Australia. This fish, which occurs only in dune lakes and swamps in wallum country, is the most common species in Fraser Island lakes. The upper Noosa River, and some freshwater streams of Fraser Island, provide significant habitats for Australian bass (*Macquarie novemaculeata*), a species whose distribution and abundance have been dramatically reduced elsewhere since European settlement.

The invertebrate fauna of the perched dune lakes is low in both diversity and numbers when compared with other freshwater lakes, but is of great scientific interest. The most primitive Chironomid (*Diptera*) larva yet known in the world occurs in great abundance in the fine sands from Lake Boomanjin on Fraser Island. Researchers discovered a new genus of the insect in Fraser Island's lakes which have a significant Gondwana connection because the subfamily Aphroteminae had previously only been known from South Africa and the tip of South America.

At least twelve new species of invertebrates have been found in the dune lakes (Insecta, Cladocera, an oligochaete worm). Even among the highly mobile dragonflies there are two species unique to the dune lakes. Other invertebrates occur in abundance only in these lakes, among them the zooplanktonic copepod *Calamoecia tasmanica*.

SOIL FAUNA

The sandmasses provide a rare medium for two specialised groups of fauna — sand swimmers that move through the sand, such as crickets and earthworms, and others that crawl across the sand surface, such as cockroaches and ants. Such fauna seems to be generally unaffected by the surface plant communities. Earthworms and ants play a significant role in the ecosystems of the dunes, and the sandmasses of south-east Queensland harbour a rich endemic earthworm fauna.

The presence of earthworms in sand podzols is in itself a most unusual phenomenon, possibly unique. Many of the species found at Cooloola appear to be the product of localised evolution and are characterised by very limited distributions and small population sizes. As such they may be endangered even by small-scale human interference.

*T*here are enormous populations of ants in the Great Sandy Region. These inhabit a mangrove, while most are sand swimmers. The region has a great diversity of ant species.

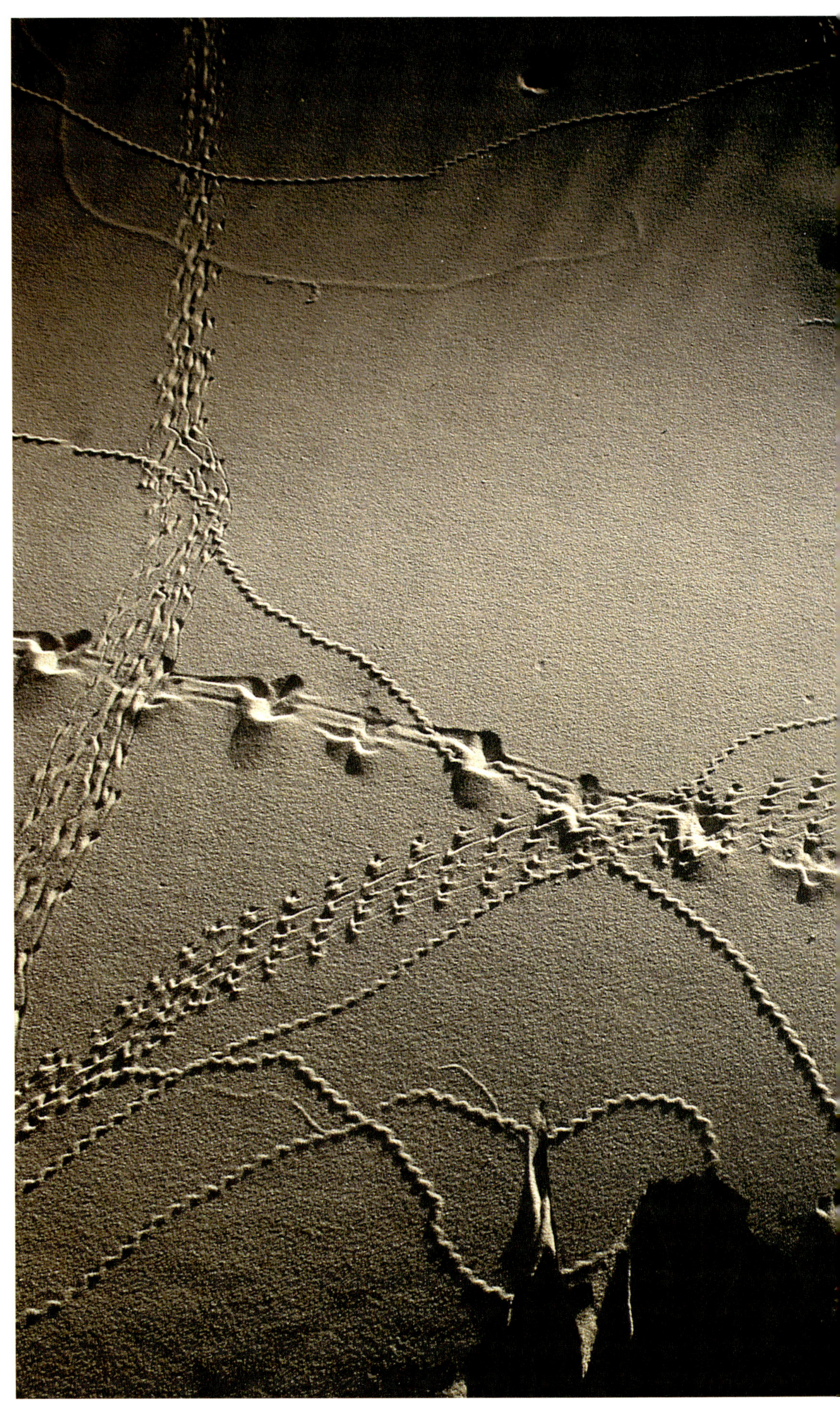

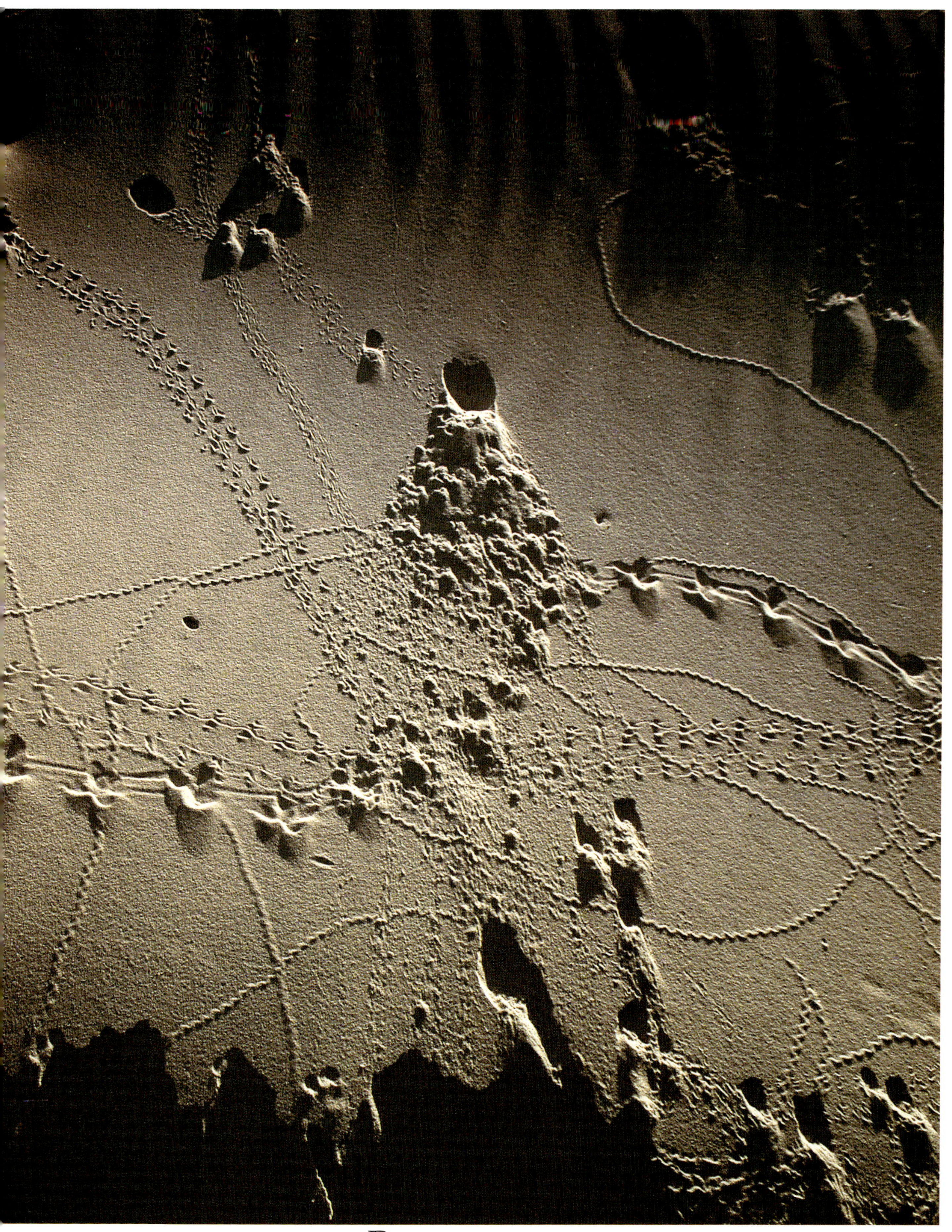

*E*arthworms, ants and other burrowing invertebrates find sand a suitable medium.

Some twenty species of earthworms have recently been recorded from the Cooloola sandmass, all but one of which are new to science. Of over five genera, one, *Pheretimoides*, is endemic to the sandmasses of south-east Queensland. One of the more spectacular species, the deep-burrowing earthworm (*Digaster keastii*), reaches a length of more than 80 centimetres, and is widespread in the coastal sandmasses and adjacent inland area. Other earthworm species parallel the acid frogs in being adapted to the high acidity levels on localised peaty habitats in the sandmasses.

It is believed that the Cooloola region may contain the greatest diversity and number of ant species so far recorded in a given area. There are over 300 ant species belonging to about fifty-five genera. There are also twenty species of termites, two of which appear to be new to science, and fifty-seven species of Collembola (springtails), five of which have apparently never been recorded before. The region contains a cricket-like creature new to science, discovered in 1980. It has been named *Cooloola propator* and placed in a new scientific family called Cooloolidae.

A giant subterranean cockroach (*Geoscapheus primulatus*), approximately 6 to 8 centimetres long and the second largest cockroach yet recorded in the world, is found in the sand dunes of the Great Sandy Region. Other active members of the dune communities, which have not been studied in detail, include burrowing bees, snails and, in certain places, freshwater crayfish.

ESTUARINE AND MARINE FAUNA

Humpback whales migrate north through waters adjacent to Cooloola and Fraser Island in early winter to breed in the waters of the southern Great Barrier Reef. Of approximately 1200 in this group, about 200 enter Hervey Bay after their calving period as they return to their Antarctic feeding ground. They remain for only a few days. The whales have been recorded between mid-August and mid-October before moving south. They do not appear to eat during their sojourn in Hervey Bay. While they are in the Bay the whales attract more than 20 000 tourists who make day trips to observe them playing and cavorting close to Fraser Island in Platypus Bay.

*H*ervey Bay is recognised as a vitally significant habitat in the migration of humpback whales (*Megaptera novaeangliae*).

The sheltered waters of the region also support several species of marine turtles and mammals, including dolphins. Hervey Bay and the Great Sandy Strait is the habitat for more than 2000 dugong (*Dugong dugon*), which is recognised as an endangered species. This is the most important Australian habitat south of Cape York for the legendary mammal, renowned as the mermaid of the sea. Thousands of sea turtles have been recorded in Hervey Bay. The turtle rookery at Mon Repos on the western side of Hervey Bay is regarded as one of the most significant on mainland Australia, attracting 300 to 400 females annually. Mon Repos is one of the most important rookeries in the world for the loggerhead sea turtle (*Caretta caretta*).

Within the Great Sandy Strait there are small natural coral reefs and a very large artificial reef. Coral reefs also occur offshore from Sandy Cape and Waddy Point and on the western side of Hervey Bay, near Bundaberg. At

The tail of one of more than 800 humpback whales which visit Hervey
Bay between August and October on their southward migration from
their Great Barrier Reef breeding grounds.

*S*oldier crabs at Wathumba Creek.

*J*ellyfish at Hook Point.

*H*ook Point beach. Sunset illuminates the littering jellyfish.

Rooney Point, divers have discovered some rare colonies of vernotid gastropods, sedentary marine snails, in a remote and rarely visited subtidal reef lying in about 30 metres of water. Large reef conglomerations of these creatures are unusual in Australia, and they are normally found only in intertidal areas. The gastropod colonies, which could be more than 100 years old, appear as a series of brown domes lying in a shallow sand depression. They are affected by strong tidal currents.

The waters adjacent to Fraser Island, Rainbow and Teewah beaches and in the Noosa River are popular with amateur anglers. In particular the ocean beach of Fraser Island attracts large numbers of enthusiasts suitably equipped with beach transport. With the exception of the upper Noosa River the same waters support a number of commercial fishing operations. Most of the commercial catch is made up of finned fish, particularly mullet, whiting, tailor, bream, mackerel and flathead, but Queensland mud crabs and prawns are also taken, mainly in estuarine and inshore areas.

The estuaries and shallow bays of the Great Sandy Strait, Tin Can Bay and the Noosa River support a rich and varied fauna. The brackish water, shallow flats, seagrass and mangrove-lined shores provide habitats for marine life, particularly juvenile fish and crustaceans. The productivity of mangrove and adjacent seagrass flats in terms of organic food production has been shown to be equal to, or greater than, that of the best farmlands. These areas produce much of the food of the fish and crustaceans of the estuary.

The large Aboriginal middens are testimony to the traditional productivity of the estuaries. During the early part of this century a ship called weekly to collect the huge oysters from the Great Sandy Strait and take them to Brisbane. The mangroves, particularly the *Rhizophora* species, are particularly important as a habitat of the famous Queensland mud crabs, one of the gastronomic delicacies of the state.

A soldier crab, one of the many armies that inhabit the Wathumba Creek estuary.

*D*awn fishers at Orchid beach are hunting tailor, a fish which local Aborigines called *dhailli*.

Facing page

*R*ed mangroves (*Rhizophora marina*) provide a habitat for the famous Queensland mud crabs.

FIGHTING TO THE FUTURE

*C*onservation aims to preserve options for the future. The history of the conservation of Fraser Island and Cooloola provides an insight into how vested interests have vigorously resisted the indefatigable efforts of those who have sought to protect the pristine wilderness values of the region.

The campaigns to protect Fraser Island from exploiters have been going on for almost a century. In 1893 it was recommended that the whole of the island should be one of three outstanding natural areas of Australia to be declared a national park. The movement to conserve both Fraser Island and Cooloola has continued since then, becoming more intense and vocal from the early 1970s. The advocacy for environmental protection has been persistently resisted by both vested interests and the Queensland government.

The Cooloola campaign and the fight for Fraser Island have had separate but parallel histories. The action to protect Cooloola has been led by two conservation groups: the Noosa Parks Association began the campaign in the early 1960s, and the Cooloola Committee led the Brisbane-based campaign from 1970 until 1989. Principal figures in this continuing campaign have included Dr Arthur Harrold, Bill and Mavis Huxley, and many others. The fight for Fraser Island has been led since January 1971 by the Fraser Island Defenders Organisation, better known by its acronym FIDO, the watchdog of Fraser Island.

Above
*O*cean Lake, Fraser Island.

Left
*E*landa Point, Lake Cootharaba.

*C*liffs of coloured sand on Fraser Island.

*T*he sweep of the zeta curve at Marloo Bay adjacent to Orchid beach is subject to active erosion and natural reshaping of the coastline by the elements.

Facing page

*T*he coloured sands on Cathedral beach have been moulded into sculptural forms.

THE COOLOOLA CONTROVERSY

Cooloola has been the centre of a continuing conservation controversy for almost three decades. It began when one of Queensland's earliest conservation groups, the Noosa Parks (Development) Association, led by Dr Harrold, saw the need for more national parks in the region. The association urged Cooloola's dedication in the early 1960s. At about the same time sandminers were assessing Cooloola's mineralisation and applying for mining leases. These applications were subsequently withdrawn in the face of vigorous opposition. In the meantime, the sandminers began a new operation on the Inskip Point peninsula on leases which they had obtained before there was any organised conservation movement. They established a mining plant and the beginnings of Rainbow Beach township in 1965. This operation, while transforming the Inskip Point peninsula, gave them a political springboard for making inroads into Cooloola proper and Fraser Island.

In 1969, after a lot of political lobbying, the miners decided to try to override Noosa Parks Association opposition in Cooloola. They lodged fresh applications for mining leases and began a battle which involved in turn the Gympie mining warden, strong Queensland public opinion, the backbench members of the Queensland parliament, state Cabinet, the Supreme Court and the Privy Council. Ultimately the miners lost at great cost.

The Noosa Parks Association was rapidly reinforced by a number of other conservation groups. Following the mining warden's hearing in 1970,

which resulted in a recommendation for mining, the Cooloola Committee, a coalition of conservation groups, was formed. The committee persuaded a majority of backbench members of the government parties to oppose the approval of the mining warden and Cabinet's recommendation that sandmining should go ahead. Reluctantly, the Queensland government resolved that there would be no sandmining on any part of Cooloola.

Pressure then mounted for the whole of Cooloola to be dedicated as a national park. This struggle continues because the objective has not yet been fully achieved, largely due to the resistance of timber interests. The Forestry Department had threatened to clearfell the pristine areas in the catchment of the Noosa River, transforming them into alien exotic pine plantations. This led to a concerted campaign to add the Womalah landscape to the Cooloola National Park.

In 1980 the Queensland government commissioned the Department of Ecosystem Management at the University of New England to prepare a report on the suitability of the upper Noosa River catchment for pine plantations. The report argued overwhelmingly in favour of retaining it for nature conservation, partly because it contained unique vegetation and environmentally sensitive areas, but also because it had a high susceptibility to erosion. Soon afterwards, the Queensland National Parks and Wildlife Service purchased 10 000 hectares of former wallum land near Maryborough as an alternative planting area for the Forestry Department. In 1983 the Womalah landscape was added to the Cooloola National Park as pine planting began 60 kilometres north on a much more suitable area. The Commonwealth government purchased Elanda Plains in 1974 for nature conservation. In 1983 this was transferred to the Queensland government to enlarge the Cooloola National Park. Several hundred hectares of vacant crown land east of Lake Cootharaba were also included in the park.

The salamander-shaped Cooloola National Park proclaimed by a government infamous for contriving curious electoral boundaries does not contain the bulk of Cooloola's tall forests. The absence of the core has long rankled conservationists, who continue efforts to preserve these critical forests and to ensure uniform management for the whole of Cooloola.

Cooloola campaigners have addressed a wide range of management issues, including opposing the building of resorts, stopping further mining operations, developing a management plan and extending the boundaries of the national park. Theirs has been a campaign of epic proportions. By their diligent and unrelenting efforts, they have been able to protect many of the natural features of Cooloola for future generations. There is, however, still much more to be preserved.

THE FIGHT FOR FRASER ISLAND

As pointed out in Chapter 3, the timber industry held total control over almost the whole of Fraser Island for more than a century. The Maryborough timber industry has steadfastly resisted all efforts to wrest the island from its

*T*he contrasting colours of wildflowers in bloom in Cooloola National Park.

*N*ear the Kinaba Information Centre, the Noosa River flows peacefully
between thickly vegetated banks.

control. This has included Aboriginal claims, moves to create a national park and even a move to give it to Nauruan sovereignty.

The Australian Association for the Advancement of Science first proposed to declare the whole of Fraser Island a national park in 1893. This nomination established a very early recognition of the unique natural values and aesthetic quality of the island. In 1961 it was proposed to resettle the Nauruan people on Fraser Island to compensate them for the desecration of their homeland by phosphate miners. Timber interests vigorously opposed this proposal but the official reason for denying the Nauruan claim was that the Fraser Island soil was too sandy for agriculture.

From 1963, events moved rapidly. Sawmillers allowed the Forestry Department to make concessions provided that they did not threaten their most lucrative source of timber. Sir Reginald Barnwall was seeking to establish the Orchid Beach tourist resort and other private citizens were applying for occupational permits on which to build holiday houses. This led to the government excising from the state forest a strip of land one kilometre wide from Eurong to Sandy Cape. The Lands Department, now responsible for that land, immediately began to subdivide and sell land at Happy Valley and Eurong. Many squatters' selections were validated during this process. A tourist development lease was allowed at the erosion-prone Orchid Beach. No environmental assessments were made in these ad hoc decisions.

In 1966 Murphyores obtained four sandmining leases covering 8665 hectares. Few people were aware of these applications or their implications. Affected landholders were unaware that their properties were included, and the lease applications were unopposed. At that time there was no organised conservation movement in the region.

After the joint government party backbenchers forced Cabinet to back down over sandmining in Cooloola in August 1970, Cabinet was determined to ensure that conservation pressure would never again frustrate the Cabinet will in Queensland. Its approach was to commission a superficial land use study to validate all proposed sandmining. In November 1970 an eight-person committee visited Fraser Island for a 45-hour evaluation. The committee was guided by a sandmining employee. No submissions from the public were invited, and no representations from conservationists were allowed. The committee endorsed the perpetuation of the existing mining leases, but ignored what the government should do about future applications.

The Cooloola sandmining controversy raised conservation consciousness and led to a determination to protect Fraser Island. Conservationists called a public meeting at Hervey Bay in September 1970 to discuss protection of the island. Sandminers from Rainbow Beach stacked the meeting, outvoting the conservationists, but some useful lessons were learned.

In January 1971 a consortium of the Australian company, Murphyores, and the American industrial giant, Dillingham, pressed its claims with a further four sandmining lease applications. Three local conservation groups agreed that a single committee should be formed to oppose these applications, and the Fraser Island Defenders Organisation came into being. FIDO at once

*C*hristmas orchids in bloom on Fraser Island.

Facing page

*N*ear Wanggoolba Creek at Central Station the rainforest is dense and a profusion of ferns and epiphytes struggle towards the life-giving light.

enlisted the support of the Australian Conservation Foundation, and the battle began in earnest. In the face of strong opposition, the mining consortium forfeited two claims near the Sandy Cape lighthouse, which had been intended to become silica quarries, but pressed on with its other claims to mine heavy minerals.

After a fourteen-day hearing, the mining warden, an employee of the Mines Department, recommended that the leases be granted. FIDO's counsel, Lew Wyvill, drew attention to legal deficiencies in the presentation of the sandminer's case, but these points were ignored. The warden had recommended in favour of sandmining and the Queensland Cabinet immediately adopted the recommendation. Four years later, the High Court of Australia found that the mining warden's interpretation of the 'public interest' was misconceived. In December 1971 Queensland Titanium Mines Pty Ltd (QTM), which had exhausted most of the resources on the Inskip Point peninsula, began a mining operation on Fraser Island's sensitive foredunes between North Spit and Eurong.

FIDO continued to mobilise opinion to ensure that such blatant political abuses were not repeated. In 1974 QTM applied for four new mining leases without any environmental assessments. For legal reasons, FIDO's objection was lodged in the name of John Sinclair. This objection was supported by 3500 petitioners, whose letters to the warden were wholly disregarded. Although FIDO's evidence went unchallenged and QTM presented virtually no evidence as to its capacity to proceed, the mining warden found in QTM's favour, saying that Sinclair had not shown that he represented the 'public interest' as a whole.

FIDO supported the Sinclair appeal to the Queensland Supreme Court, but the appeal was unanimously rejected. The appeal then went to the High Court of Australia. In May 1975 the full bench unanimously upheld the appeal and in doing so, defined the 'public interest' for future deliberations in common law. The High Court judgement stated that one person can be held to represent the public interest.

In 1973 two other important initiatives began. Land development proposals were submitted for two or three larger Fraser Island freehold land holdings — the first was at Wathumba Creek, an area of 65 hectares entirely surrounded by the new national park. Despite the indifference of the local government, FIDO managed to frustrate the various subdivision proposals. Likewise, FIDO ensured that the Lands Department did not undertake further subdivision of Fraser Island at Eurong or Happy Valley. However, as a result of rezoning in 1983, FIDO was not able to pursue its objections to the new subdivision that proceeded at Orchid Beach.

As a result of these controversies, Fraser Island had already gained some notoriety by 1973. Because the issues on Fraser Island epitomised many Australian land-use conflicts, the Committee of Inquiry into the National Estate spent four days on a FIDO safari in 1973. In November of the following year Prime Minister Whitlam went to Fraser Island as a guest of various developers. The Dillingham–Murphyores sandmining operations were

*L*ake Cootharaba at Boreen Point.

exempted from the provisions of the newly passed Environmental Protection (Impact of Proposals) Act, 1974. When Dillingham began constructing mining plant in February 1975, FIDO suspected that something was wrong. In March the public was finally told that export contracts had been promised. FIDO and the Australian Conservation Foundation then successfully campaigned for an environmental inquiry.

After opening on 2 June 1975, the commissioners spent six days inspecting Fraser Island and three weeks sitting in Maryborough. The sandmining companies withdrew from the hearing after a few days and, with the Queensland government, refused to co-operate with the inquiry. They challenged the validity of the inquiry in the High Court. On 5 August 1975, after being given new terms of reference, a second inquiry, under the same commissioners, began in Brisbane. Seventy-four witnesses gave evidence and 658 exhibits were tendered.

After waiting a year until the High Court upheld the inquiry's validity, the commissioners handed down their final report and recommendations on 21 October 1976. There were only three recommendations:

> 1 All exports of minerals (including minerals that have been subjected to processing or treatment) extracted or which may hereafter be extracted from Fraser Island be absolutely prohibited except for minerals extracted from below the mean high-water mark on the eastern beach south of Indian Head:
>
> 2 Appropriate economic and other assistance be given to the extent that adverse regional economic effects follow the implementation of Recommendation 1:
>
> 3 The whole of Fraser Island be recorded as part of the National Estate as soon as possible.

A sandblow, advancing at the speed of a glacier, is at least as powerful in shaping the regional landscape.

*T*he estuary and wetlands of Wathumba Creek. The complex
interaction of ocean, river, sand and vegetation has created the unique
environment of the Great Sandy Region.

*P*atterns in the sand are evidence of sand bubbler crabs.

The Australian government, after consulting with the Queensland government, announced the adoption of all the report's recommendations on 10 November 1976. On 18 November Fraser Island became the first item to be listed on the Register of the National Estate. Sandmining concluded on Fraser Island at the end of 1976. The sandmining companies and first line contractors were offered $5 million in ex-gratia payments and $10 million was provided to the Queensland government by the Commomwealth government to offset regional unemployment.

Although $1 million of the ex-gratia payments was accepted by QTM and various contractors, Dillingham–Murphyores declined a $4 million offer, demanding instead $23.9 million as compensation for an expropriated asset.

The Commonwealth government denied that allegation. The issue was disputed in the international arena with the United States government backing Dillingham's claims until 1982. Murphyores' mining leases remained intact on Fraser Island and in 1984 the company negotiated to exchange some for real estate on the Inskip Point peninsula. In 1987 the Queensland government secretly renewed the remaining Fraser Island leases for a further twenty-one years. Murphyores has declared that it will resume sandmining on Fraser Island as soon as the Commonwealth administrative export embargo is lifted.

A CONTINUING BATTLE

When sandmining ceased most people saw it as a victory for conservation and assumed that thereafter Fraser Island was safe. Few were aware that the whole island is not a national park and that there continues to be devastating logging of the island's National Estate forests. The controversy over sandmining caused an unprecedented increase in tourism to Fraser Island. FIDO then focused on the future long-term management of Fraser Island, to enable maximum usage without depreciation from pressures of human population.

In 1975 FIDO had commissioned the first management study ever undertaken for Fraser Island. Prepared by Mr J. P. Stanton, that study is still regarded as one of the landmark studies of the island. In 1978 the Co-ordinator General prepared a management study for the Queensland government without inviting any public comment or input. FIDO responded by preparing and submitting its own management strategy. FIDO's submissions were not incorporated into the government's plan, which allowed continued logging and the resumption of sandmining. However, the Queensland government did not implement its own plan. Instead, ministers continued to make ad hoc decisions which resulted in many ill-advised and incompatible developments. Despite the government's attempts to muzzle FIDO this organisation strongly opposed such actions, even appealing to the Supreme Court which yet again upheld the right of Queensland government ministers to proceed unfettered.

In 1985 the government conceded that the island was in a mess by establishing the Fraser Island Recreation Board to address the management of recreation. This was to be financed on the user-pays principle which

Waddy Point is a favourite haunt for fishers and a launching base for
deep-sea fishing boats.

*E*xperiments in the 1920s tried to replace the Fraser Island rainforest with plantations of hoop pine. The damage resulting from rainforest exploitation and other logging is a continuing source of controversy.

Facing page
*M*elaleuca or paperbark trees have survived the often rapacious onslaughts of loggers, and ancient trees still stand firm by the lakes.

*A*n elkhorn and profusely growing fishbone ferns thrive in the Fraser Island rainforest. They are among the most common epiphytes of the forest.

introduced fees for national park services for the first time in Queensland. On 28 November 1986, National Parks Minister Peter McKechnie announced that a new recreation management plan was to be developed for the government: 'The management plan will provide a basis for future orderly development and co-ordinated manner of outdoor recreation on Fraser Island.'

FIDO updated its previous management strategy to produce a further detailed submission. However, the government's Fraser Island Recreation Management Plan allowed the continuation of logging and the resumption of sandmining. In addition ministers continued to make decisions that negated the positive aspects of the management plan. They supported an exponential growth in tourism on the island and aided the development of a 2200-bed resort at North White Cliffs in an unstable area subject to a serious sand-slide.

In an attempt to placate conservationists in 1971, when the government decided to allow further sandmining, a national park was declared at the northern end of Fraser Island. It contained 23 000 hectares. The National Parks and Wildlife Service failed to pursue the government's recommendation that it make the area around Lake Boomanjin and Lake Birrabeen a national park. The park was increased to 32 400 hectares in a second instalment in 1973, and has been subsequently increased to 52 400 hectares. Although a 40-kilometre strip of mining leases which prevented the national park reaching the beach was surrendered, the sacrosanctity of the national park concept was corrupted in 1974, when sandminers were given leases within the park to store processed minerals and machinery.

Because of loggers' demands for access to the largest and most magnificent trees, the most outstanding aesthetic features of Fraser Island, particularly its lakes and rainforest, have been left out of the national park. The present Great Sandy National Park does not include most of the popular scenic areas of the island, most of the spectacular perched dune lakes, the best forests or any of the coastline or marine areas of the Great Sandy Strait. The most beautiful spots, including Wabby Lakes, lakes Boomanjin and McKenzie, and Wanggoolba and Eli creeks, are outside the national park. In short, it contains only those parts of the island not wanted by land and tourist developers, sandminers or timber interests.

A further facet in the 'dismember, divide and exploit' philosophy has been the involvement of local government. After years of agitation by Hervey Bay interests, the Queensland government established a Local Government Boundaries Tribunal in 1974. The tribunal recommended that Fraser Island continue to share the same local authority as the Hervey Bay township. The Ministry of Local Government, concerned that the new Hervey Bay Council may frustrate the timber and sandmining interests, determined that the whole of Fraser Island should go to the exploitation-oriented Maryborough City Council. There was an enormous outcry as Hervey Bay citizens sought to reclaim Fraser Island, as a result of which the administration of Fraser Island was split in half. The northern half went to Hervey Bay and the southern half, with its critical mineral resources, went to Maryborough.

*L*ake Boomanjin. The purity of its waters could be threatened by
pollution and uncontrolled tourism, but the lake remains outside the
Great Sandy National Park.

Facing page

*S*unset over the reeds, as dusk settles on Fraser Island.

After being managed almost exclusively by a single authority for a century until 1963, within a decade management of Fraser Island was split up between six government agencies (the departments of Forestry, Lands, Mines and Tourism, the Beach Protection Authority, National Parks and Wildlife Service) and two local authorities, as well as a multiplicity of small landholders. Fraser Island was transformed from a singular well-managed entity to a mutilated, randomly developed hotch potch. This had the effect of reducing the level of management to something approaching anarchy.

THE LOSS OF WILDERNESS

Judith Wright, one of Australia's leading poets, described the qualities of wilderness of the Great Sandy Region to the Fraser Island Environmental Inquiry in 1975:

> These are the qualities of wilderness — the qualities of the ocean-side wilderness — which Fraser Island does particularly represent and the water, the lakes and the rainforest, which Patrick White describes so well. They give a sense of awe, I think, of sensitivity towards the landscape . . . I know very few children — urban children — who have been able to experience, as people of my age did, the joy of loneliness on a coastline, of beauty experienced without human interference.

*F*oxtail sedges (*Caustis blakeii*) thrive in the moist conditions near Lake Boomanjin.

*M*ost visitors to Fraser Island use the ferry services between Inskip
Point and Hook Point on the southern end of the island.

*F*our-wheel-drives have
unwittingly eroded the
wilderness values of the Great
Sandy Region, a process
exacerbated by taming the
wildlife and feeding feral horses.

Since Judith Wright first visited Fraser Island in 1947 to form that assessment
of the wilderness values of the Great Sandy Region, they have been progressively eroded away. The challenge of isolation is being lost, and the breaking
down of that remoteness from civilisation brings more than a twinge of
nostalgia to those who knew the region before then.

Because of poor access, and a lack of appreciation of its aesthetic qualities
and wilderness values, tourism on Fraser Island developed very slowly. A
resort was commenced during the 1930s at Happy Valley, but failed because
of the economic depression. Until the 1960s there was no Rainbow Beach
settlement, or even a road to Rainbow Beach; there was no Eurong village,
Orchid Beach resort or Dilli village. Happy Valley was just a small, shabby
collection of fishing shacks. Once established, these settlements expanded
rapidly. Simultaneously the region was being vigorously explored for its
mineral potential. Sandmining degraded a small area but left an infrastructure
which opportunists quickly exploited. At the same time the insatiable timber
industry was probing further and deeper into the forest. The increasing
popularity of off-road vehicles helped many thousands more to gain indepen-
dent access to the region.

Until about 1965, the only regular weekly boat service to Fraser Island
was run by the Forestry Department launch, *Korawinga*. Now there are
several vehicular ferries running continuously seven days a week and at least
four tourist launches providing scheduled daily services. First came more
ferries; then came more people; then came shops, ice supplies and two hotels

A lone fisher enjoys the surf near Indian Head.

on Fraser Island; another hotel, several motels and even a waterslide at Rainbow Beach and an expanded community and infrastructure. After that came petty larceny, stolen vehicles and vandalism.

Then came the police to control this lawless frontier and to attempt to establish law and order and adherence to traffic rules on the beaches. Still the accident rate continued to rise. Rescue facilities were the first line of defence. A contingency plan for helicopter rescue was developed. Then Telecom upgraded telecommunications and provided an automatic telephone link between the Great Sandy Region and the outside world. New bushfire brigades and first-aid posts were established. The hardy self-reliance that people needed not long ago is rapidly disappearing. One recent visitor claimed that Fraser Island was 'having the heart ripped out of it by fat-bellied, four wheel driving, beer drinking cowboys . . . [exhibiting] drunkenness, foul language, filth and totally uncontrolled behaviour'.

In 1985 litter could be found at nearly every abandoned camp site. The long-term damage to the foredunes was even more obvious. Extensive areas were denuded of vegetation. Trees around all popular camp sites had been thinned or stripped for campfire wood. Ground cover had been churned up by the ubiquitous four-wheel-drives which had probed into the foredunes every hundred metres or so. Grass was dead from a succession of camps on the same site. Almost every patch of foredune suitable for tent sites had been mauled and indelibly scarred. Another problem is sewage disposal. Septic tanks rapidly become sealed up by organic matter in the same way that the floors of perched dune lakes become sealed and impervious when organic matter mixes with wet sand.

Domestic dogs passed on the debilitating *Parvo* virus to the dingoes and threatened to hybridise with them. Brumbies have had an adverse impact on the foredunes, causing more damage than previously appreciated. Feral cattle were ordered to be removed from Fraser Island under the TB and brucellosis eradication campaign, but some escaped the 1985 round-up. The introduction of the exotic boneseed weed to the once-mined Inskip Point–Rainbow Beach area has unleashed potentially Australia's worst scourge of sand dunes. Other exotic weeds have invaded the region, depreciating its natural values.

The mouth of Wanggoolba Creek was the site of one of the first forestry operations during the period between 1917 and 1920. In the 1950s the creek was one of the main access points for either boats or aircraft, although boats could not navigate the shallow tortuous channel except near full tide, and even then only with extreme caution. In 1984 the Queensland parliament revoked part of the Maaroom Fisheries Habitat Reserve to allow dredging near the mouth of Wanggoolba Creek. The all-weather, all-tide access was achieved at considerable environmental cost and with further loss of wilderness values.

The Great Sandy Strait has so far evaded the predatory pressure that has been focused on other major coastal estuaries in Queensland and made them targets for canal construction and other drastic modifications. Changes to the status of the islands and the four villages flanking the strait may mean the

*B*ooiungan Rocks Bypass. Convoys of vehicles cross the sand to meet the ferries.

loss of what is a precious aquatic wilderness. What was once a quiet secluded anchorage at Garrys Camp lost its isolation in less than a decade and has become a busy sanctuary for yachts. Consequently, even on the water seclusion is now only rarely available.

Lengthy walking trails have been constructed, or are designed, for most of the length of Fraser Island and Cooloola. The Eliza Fraser trail runs from Lake Cootharaba to Poverty Point on Tin Can Bay. The Kgari trail runs almost the length of Fraser Island. Such walking trails help walkers avoid the four-wheel-drives and vehicular tracks. However, a walking track to Lake Wanhar, the largest lake on the island, erodes the immediate prospect of a trackless wilderness on the island's Top End.

In the siting of new camping areas the preservation of wilderness needs a higher priority. Today's camping grounds are equipped with showers. The creature comforts accompanying modern campers include generators for refrigerators and lighting plants. Now mains power is being sought even for remote sites on Fraser Island.

Corduroy tracks to bypass rocks make it easier to travel the beaches in all weather and at all tides. They also mean that there is now little respite from the procession of vehicles, even at high tide. The amenity for motorists is impacting heavily on the amenity of pedestrians. Subdivision in the Great Sandy Region is generally inappropriate. Since 1963 creeping settlement has been stealing into new parts of the region despite intense opposition from conservationists attempting to preserve the remaining wilderness qualities.

Gone are the pioneering adventurous expeditions described by Judith Wright. Referring to her trip to Fraser Island in about 1947 she said:

I went across on one of the timber loading boats from Maryborough. There was almost no access to Fraser Island for tourists at that time and I worked my way across as cook and tied up in a mangrove creek. I do not like to remember the experience of the sand flies. After leaving that area, I walked. There was almost no way of seeing the island except on foot. I walked across to the ocean beach and through a good deal of the rainforest and it was an extraordinary experience for me. I had not been long in Queensland, I had not seen the kind of landscape that the north coastal Queensland areas offered at all. It was my first experience of rainforest itself and I found it very moving indeed, and I would say that at that time walking through Fraser Island was a more exciting experience in its then more or less untouched state than driving across it was the last time I went.

Of course, when you are walking, when you are actually camping in a place, you do have an experience of it that cannot be provided when you are in a vehicle, which is one reason why I think that the wilderness experience of Fraser Island should be preserved and that access should be more by personal experience. That, I have never forgotten, more particularly, as I think during my whole three days on the island we met only three people and they were all Forestry employees.

*K*inaba Information Centre — the main access point to the upper Noosa River — sees more than 90 000 visitors annually pass through by boat and canoe.

*B*irdlife is disturbed by a constant procession of visitors.

The accelerated degradation of the Great Sandy Region has been accepted by a largely apathetic public who have not appreciated that it is a series of small decisions that enables wilderness to slip away. Widening and gravelling roads, draping wire-scapes of power lines, building Telecom towers, camping areas, trails, resorts and introducing entry fees and permits are all examples of the pernicious loss of wilderness. In the Great Sandy Region there are many people who do appreciate wilderness values but they have been, so far, powerless in helping to retain them.

In 1974 Fraser Island was one of the first four areas of Australia to be considered by the Australian Conservation Foundation as worthy of World Heritage nomination. The other three areas (the Great Barrier Reef, southwest Tasmania and Kakadu) have already been listed. Lord Howe Island, recommended in 1975, is now also on this prestigious list.

In 1984 FIDO and the Australian Conservation Foundation prepared a World Heritage nomination for the Great Sandy Region. The submission showed that the whole region measures up to World Heritage nomination criteria on all four grounds: physical dimensions and geomorphic attributes, cultural significance, biological significance and outstanding aesthetic quality. Paranoia about World Heritage has to date enabled the Queensland government to exercise a virtual de facto right of veto by ignoring the nomination.

MANAGEMENT PRINCIPLES

FIDO's objectives for Fraser Island apply equally to the whole of the Great Sandy Region. The association wants the management practices for the region to retain the maximum natural biological diversity, cultural and aesthetic values and wilderness quality, and to allow as much recreation as is compatible with the retention of the region's outstanding natural values.

To achieve this aim FIDO listed ten objectives:

1 The Great Sandy Region should be recognised as a unique part of the world's cultural and natural heritage. As one of the wonders of the world, its management should be directed towards maximising the benefits of that World Heritage status and preserving its integrity.
2 All crown land in the region should be given inviolable national park status and, in the interim, the management should be so as not to depreciate the natural values.
3 Land uses incompatible with the aim should be eliminated. This means that logging would cease and sandmining would be ruled out as a future option.
4 Preservation of wilderness values should be one of the highest priorities for the management. Wilderness, where the natural environment is untrammelled by humans and where humans are only visitors, would mean that the lowest environmental impact in the recreational usage of visitors and residents would be permitted. In a modern technological society one of the scarcest commodities is wilderness which provides solitude, physical and mental challenge, a place for scientific study, inspiration, and primitive recreation for present and future generations.

*B*oardwalks have been erected to reduce the environmental impact of thousands of trampling feet on the fragile dunes. The first boardwalk at Eli Creek, built by the Fraser Island Defenders Organisation, provided a model now repeated elsewhere.

5 The volume of visitors to particular areas should be limited to a level which is consistent with the carrying capacity of the area.

6 Urbanisation within the region should be limited in both area and population. The permanent resident population should be kept to the minimum necessary for management purposes and recreational use should be based outside the defined area.

7 Management should be directed towards allowing as much of the region as possible to revert as far as possible to true wilderness. To this end factors which would depreciate the area's wilderness value should be phased out as soon as possible. Any new developments incompatible with wilderness should be located outside the protected area of the region and any existing developments should be relocated outside it.

8 Where any developments are permitted in accordance with proper environmental impact studies subject to proper evaluation and modification, measures must be taken to ensure that the environmental impact is minimised. FIDO believes that wherever possible any new work developments occur on areas already degraded rather than degrade new areas.

9 Economic criteria should not outweigh biological, cultural, aesthetic and other natural values in any management decisions.

10 Public participation and involvement should be permitted at all stages of planning, evaluation of environmental impact studies and management plans. A representative of the voluntary conservation movement should be included in any major deliberations relating to management.

A TEN-POINT VISITOR CODE

This ten-point code has been developed to enable visitors to the Great Sandy Region to have a minimum impact on this precious, fragile and enchanting natural environment.

1 *Carry in and out.* This is the most obvious rule to avoid littering. Yet it is thoughtlessly neglected or disregarded by the mindless monsters of our throwaway society, who discard cans and bottles and then provide visual pollution or leave their litter for others to dispose of. Whether on foot, in motor vehicles or by boat, all garbage should be taken away for disposal outside the region. So whether a package, bottle or can is empty or not, it should be carried out. Although some substances are biodegradable this takes time, and during that time they are untidy and smelly.

2 *Don't deface the coloured sand or vegetation.* Both are protected by law and a prosecution could result. However, all people should voluntarily strive to preserve beauty rather than be deterred by law enforcement procedures to see that the region is not degraded for others. Climbing on the coloured sand cliffs or engraving initials on them accelerates erosion.

3 *Don't pick wildflowers.* It is illegal to remove any vegetation from state forests or national parks without a special permit.

4 *Observe careful sanitation procedures in your camping.* Dig deep holes for toilet purposes and ensure that the site is identified as a former toilet so that others

*T*he erosion of the coloured sand cliffs at Rainbow beach has been exacerbated by greater human pressure.

won't camp too close. Be careful to ensure that drainage from camp sites does not cause pollution.

5 *Don't use soap in the lakes or streams.* This pollutes and changes the chemical composition of the water. In most cases additives are not necessary because the water is so soft. Protect the quality of some of the purest naturally occurring water in the world. Do not urinate in the lakes. There should be no camping or driving of any motor vehicles within 100 metres of any lake and no power boats are permitted on any lakes.

6 *Fire must be strictly controlled.* Use proper fireplaces where these are provided. Where no fireplaces are provided the Rural Fires Act requires that all combustible material be cleared for 2 metres around the fire and that it be completely extinguished before it is left. Fires need not be big. Do not destroy live vegetation for firewood.

7 *Don't drive if you can walk.* Too many tracks are needlessly damaged or eroded by thoughtless people who drive very short distances when they could walk just as easily. Driving adds to traffic congestion which could be eliminated if more people took up the healthier exercise of walking. The heavy impact of traffic across the foredunes can be reduced if this rule is observed.

8 *The region is a fauna sanctuary.* Almost all the Great Sandy Region is a fauna sanctuary, and much is national park. All plants and fauna are protected. The use of firearms is absolutely prohibited. Do not feed any wild animals. Do not take any domestic pets to the region. These may carry diseases that affect native animals.

9 *Motorised vehicles should avoid erosion and undue noise.* In four-wheel-drives this is best done by controlling both speed and wheel slip and by driving in the highest gear possible for the conditions. All vehicles should have front-wheel-drive engaged at all times for safety and to cope with emergency. Boat users should be particularly careful to minimise the wash on the banks of the Noosa River. A maximum speed limit of 6.5 kilometres per hour exists on the river. Whether on the river or on the tracks, motor noises should be limited by reducing speeds and ensuring that good mufflers are fitted so that the serenity of this natural area is not unduly shattered.

10 *Respect and protect Aboriginal artefacts.* These are priceless and irreplaceable parts of Australia's national heritage. The Great Sandy Region is rich in such treasures, including middens, special trees, ceremonial grounds and artefacts. These are protected by law and must not be interfered with.

A hundred and fifty years after Aborigines were forced to abandon their tribal life in the Great Sandy Region little evidence of their 40 000-year occupation remains. What will remain in 150 years' time of 150 years of non-Aboriginal use?

*M*any visitors to the region turn their backs to the wondrous sand
dunes and watch the tips of their rods dipping towards the surf.

FURTHER READING

Alexander, M. (1971) *Mrs Fraser on the Fatal Shore*. Michael Joseph, London.

Armitage, E. F. (1926) *Reminiscences of a Queensland Pioneer*. Brisbane Technical College.

Armitage, E. F. (8 June 1929) 'Nature's bounty: seen on Fraser Island, giant monarchs of the forest, mysterious freshwater lakes'. *Maryborough Chronicle*.

Arthington, A. H. (1984) 'The freshwater fish of North Stradbroke, Moreton and Fraser Islands'. *North Stradbroke Island Papers*, Boolarong Press, Brisbane.

Arthington, A. H., Burton, H. and Williams, R. W. (1984) Effects of Drifting Sand on Lake Wabby and the Ecology of other Fraser Island Lakes.

Arthington, A. H. and Hegerl, E. J. (1988) 'The distribution, conservation status and management problems of Queensland's athlassic and tidal wetlands' in *The Conservation of Australian Wetlands*. World Wildlife Fund.

Arthington, A. H. and Watson, J. A. C. (1982) 'Dragonflies (Odonata) of eastern Queensland and north eastern New South Wales'. *Aust. J. Mar. Freshwater Res.* 33:77–88.

Australian Conservation Foundation (1974) 'Incredible Fraser Island'. *Habitat*, Special Issue.

Baverstock, F. (1985) *Fraser Island: Sands of Time*. Australian Broadcasting Corporation, Sydney.

Bayly, I. A. E., Ebsworth, E. P. and Wan Hang Fung (1975) 'Studies on the lakes of Fraser Island, Queensland, Australia'. *Aust. J. Mar. Freshwater Res.* 26:1–13.

Bayly, I. A. E. and Williams, W. D. (1973) *Inland Waters and their Ecology*. Longman, Melbourne.

Beaglehole, J. C. (1962) *The Endeavour Journal of Joseph Banks. 1768–1771*. Vol II London.

Bird, E. C. F (1974) 'Dune stability on Fraser Island'. *Queensland Naturalist* 21:1–2.

Bird, E. C. F. (1972) *Coasts: An Introduction to Systematic Geomorphology*. ANU Press, Canberra.

Bird, E. C. F (1978) 'The nature and source of beach materials on the Australian coast' in Davies, J. L. and Williams. M. A. J. (eds) *Landform evolution in Australasia*. ANU Press, Canberra, 144–57.

Breene, P. G. (ed) (1986) Environmental Impact Study for Resort at North White Cliffs. Phillip G. Greene, Consulting Engineers, Brisbane.

Brewer, R. and Thompson, C. H. (1980) 'Morphology of two sub-tropical podzols formed on a siliceous dune in coastal Queensland' in Joseph, K. T. (ed) *Proc. Conf. Class. Manag. Trop. Soils*. Malaysian Soc. Soil Science, 116–23.

Bridge, B. J. and Ross P. J. (1983) 'Water erosion in vegetated sand dunes at Cooloola, south-east Queensland'. *Z. Geomorph. Suppl.* 45:227–44.

Bridge, B. J., Ross P. J. and Thompson, C. H. (1984) 'Studies in landscape dynamics in the Cooloola — Noosa River area, Queensland'. 3. CSIRO Aust. Div. Soils Divl. Rep. No. 75.

Buchanan, W. N. (October 1979) 'The captivity and rescue of Eliza Fraser'. Gympie and District Historical Society.

Coaldrake, J. C. (1962) 'The coastal sand dunes of southern Queensland'. *Proc. R. Soc. Qd.* 72:101–16.

Coaldrake, J. E. (1961) 'Ecosystems of the coastal lowlands (Wallum) southern Queensland'. *CSIRO Bulletin*, 283.

Coaldrake, E. J. (ed) (1983) Environmental Impact Study for Proposed Upgrading of Existing Barge Facilities at Wangoolba Creek. Cameron McNamara, Brisbane.

Coaldrake, E. J. (ed) (1974) Environmental Impact Study for Proposed Development at Wathumba Inlet, Fraser Island for Fisherman's Cove Pty Ltd. by A. A. Heath and Partners Pty Ltd. and Morgan and Stanley Pty Ltd, Brisbane.

Cooke, B. N., McIntyre, N., Marsh, J. A. and Tulip, D. F. Fraser Island field study notes. Kelvin Grove College of Advanced Education.

Co-ordinator-General's Department, Queensland (1978) Fraser Island Management Plan. 2 vols. Brisbane.

CSIRO, Division of Soils. *Research Reports* 1976–80, 1981–2, 1983–4.

Curtis, J. (1888) *Shipwreck of the Sterling Castle*. London.

Dawson, A. (1977) *Early Chronicles of Cypress Land: Cooloola*. A. Dawson, Pomona.

Devitt, J. (1979) Fraser Island Aboriginal Resources and Settlement Pattern. Thesis, University of Queensland.

Division of Conservation, Parks and Wildlife (1989) *Hervey Bay: Investigation into a Marine Park*.

Don, A. (1982) *Fraser Island Tour Operators' Handbook*. Department of Forestry.

Dwyer, P. D., Kikkawa J. and Ingram, G. J. (1977) 'Habitat relations of vertebrates in subtropical heathlands in coastal South Eastern Queensland'. *Ecosystems of the World*. 9a, Descriptive Studies. Elsevier, Amsterdam.

Edwardson, W. L. (1822) Unpublished papers, Mitchell Library, Sydney.

Elsol, J. and Applegate, G. 'Fraser Island'. Field Trip 14. XIII International Botanical Congress, 1981.

Evans, R. and Walker, J. (1977) 'These strangers, where are they going?: Aboriginal–European relations in the Fraser Island and Wide Bay region. 1770–1905'. *Occasional Papers in Anthropology, 8*. Anthropology Museum, University of Queensland.

Flinders, M. (1814) '*A Voyage To Terra Australis*'. London.

Fraser Island Environmental Inquiry (1975) Transcript, exhibits and submissions.

Fraser Island Recreation Board (1988) *Recreation Management Plan for Fraser Island Recreation Area*.

Georges, A. (1983) 'Reproduction of the Australian freshwater turtle. *Emydura krefftii*. Zoological Society of London.

Gibbings, R., (1937) *John Graham — Convict*. Digit, London.

Greenslade, P. and Thompson, C. H. (1981) 'Ant distribution, vegetation and soil relationships in the Cooloola–Noosa River area, Queensland'. *Vegetation Classification in Australia*. CSIRO.

Greenslade, P. and Thompson, C. H. (1981) 'Collemba from the Cooloola Noosa Area, Queensland'. *Proceedings of the Royal Society of Queensland*, 92:11–19.

Grimes, K. G. (1982) 'Stratigraphic drilling reports: GSQ Sandy Cape 1–3R'. *Queensland Government Mining Journal*.

Harrold, A. G., Noosa Parks Association and Cooloola Committee. *The Cooloola Conflict*. Queensland Conservation Council.

Harrold, A. G., Noosa Parks Association and Cooloola Committee. *Newsletter*.

Harrold, A. G. (1977) *The Case for the Western Catchment of the Noosa River to Form Part of the Cooloola National Park*. Queensland Conservation Council.

Harrold, A. G. (1971) 'Cooloola: an Ecological Mosaic'. *Queensland Naturalist*, 20:7–14.

Heinsohn, G. E. and Wake J. A. (1976) 'The importance of the Fraser Island region to dugongs'. *Operculum*. Australian Littoral Society, 5, 1.

Hemmings, L. and B. (1981) 'Exploring Fraser Island'. GEO, 3, 2.

Hemmings, L. and B. (1984) 'Cooloola National Park: still waters, muddy future?'. GEO. 3, 3.

Hemmings, L. and Sinclair, J. (1984) *Nomination of the Great Sandy Region for inclusion on the World Heritage List*. Australian Conservation Foundation.

Hookey, J. and Hicks, A. B. (1976) *Fraser Island Environmental Inquiry: Final Report of the Commission of Inquiry*. AGPS, Canberra.

Inter-Departmental Committee Report. *Fraser Island Management Plan*. Queensland Coordinator General's Department, 1978.

Inter-Departmental Committee Report. *Survey of Fraser Island and Round Hill Head*. Queensland Coordinator General's Department, 1971.

Jarvis, S. (1975–6) Unpublished papers and statement to Fraser Island Environmental Inquiry.

Jehne, W. and Thompson, C. H. (1981) 'Endomycorrhizae in plant colonization on coastal sand-dunes at Cooloola, Queensland'. *Australian Journal of Ecology*, 6:221–30.

Kerr, J. (1975) 'Fraser Island Tramways'. *Sunshine Express Newsletter*, Queensland Railways Historical Association, Brisbane.

Kikkawa, J. and Nix, H. A. (eds) (1975) 'Managing terrestrial ecosystems'. *Proceedings of the Ecological Society of Australia*.

Lane, B. A. (1987) *Shorebirds of Australia*. Nelson, Melbourne.

Lane, B. and Jessop, A. 'National wader count and report to participants'. *Royal Australasian Ornithologists Union*, May 1983, December 1983 and May 1984.

Lauer, P. K. (1977) 'Fraser Island'. *Occasional Papers in Anthropology, 8.* Anthropology Museum, University of Queensland.

Lauer, P. K. (1978) *Occasional Papers in Anthropology, 9.* Anthropology Museum, University of Queensland.

Little, I. P., Armitage, T. M. and Gilkes, R. J. (1978) 'Weathering of quartz in dune sands under sub-tropical conditions in eastern Australia'. *Geoderma*, 20:225–237.

McDonald, G. T., Wilke, L. and Morison, J. (1984) *The Economic Significance of Cooloola.* Institute of Applied Social Research, Griffith University.

Meston, A. (1905) Report on Fraser Island, Queensland Legislative Assembly.

Noakes, R. R. (1974) 'A methodological investigation of the demand for tourism on Fraser Island and the value of resource allocation to improve supply. PhD Thesis, University of New England.

Olsen, H. F. (1980) 'Sea-grasses: occurrences and distribution'. *Queensland Fisheries Service Research Bulletin* 2:91–4.

Owens, I. G. (1975-6) Unpublished papers and statement to Fraser Island Environmental Inquiry.

Parliamentary Papers concerning Captain Kent and Fraser Island (1905)

Parliament of the Commonwealth of Australia (1983) 'Lighthouses: Do we keep the keepers?' Report from the House of Representatives Standing Committee on Expenditure.

Parsons, R. (1976) *The Port of Maryborough.* Parsons, Magill, SA

Petrie, C. C. (1904) *Early Reminiscences of Queensland.* Brisbane.

Petrie, R. S. (1978-89) Unpublished papers and articles in MOONBI, Fraser Island Defenders Organisation.

Petrie, W. R. (1916) *The Forests of Fraser Island.* Forestry Department, Brisbane.

Petrie, W. R. (1925) *Report.* Forestry Department, Brisbane.

Petrie, W. R. (1926) *A Note on Dundathu Kauri.* Forestry Department, Brisbane.

Pickett, J. W., Thompson, C. H., Kelley, R. A. and Roman D. (1984) 'Evidence on high sea level during isotope stage 5c in Queensland, Australia', *Quaternary Research* 24, 103–14.

Queensland Museum (1975) The National Estate in the Moreton and Wide Bay–Burnett Regions, South-East Queensland and Recommendations on its Management. Report for the Coordinator General.

Queensland National Parks and Wildlife Service (1979) Cooloola National Park Proposed Management Plan.

Queensland National Parks and Wildlife Service (1986) *Fraser Island Plant Checklist.* Queensland National Parks and Wildlife Service.

Reeve, R. and Fergus, I. F. (1982) 'Black and white waters and their possible relationship to the podzolization process'. *Australian Journal of Soil Research* 21:59–66.

Richards, B. N. (ed) (1976) The Utilization, Management and Conservation of the Forest Resources on Fraser Island: a Study of the Socio-Economic and Ecological Effects of Timber Getting. Report to Hune and Son Pty Ltd and Wilson Hart and Co Ltd, Maryborough.

Roffey-Mitchell, N. ed (1975) *Some Considerations of the Use and Value of Resources on Fraser Island, with Particular Reference to the Sandmining Controversy.* Dept of Biology and Environmental Science, Queensland Institute of Technology.

Royal Society of Queensland (1975) *Proceedings.* Vol. 86.

Schnierer, S. B. (1982) The biology of the Australian bass in the Richmond River, New South Wales. M.Sc. Thesis, University of Queensland.

Seymour. J. (1981-2) 'The Dunes of Cooloola'. ECOS, No. 30.

Sinclair, J. (1979) *Discovering Fraser Island*, Pacific Maps, Sydney.

Sinclair, J. (1979) *Discovering Cooloola*, Pacific Maps, Sydney.

Sinclair, J. (1978) *Fraser Island Management Strategy 1978-2000.* Fraser Island Defenders Organisation.

Sinclair, J. (1987) *Management Strategy for Fraser Island*, Fraser Island Defenders Organisation.

Sinclair, J. (1985) The Management of Queensland's Great Sandy Islands. Unpublished paper prepared for the CONCOM workshop on the management of Australia's Offshore Islands, Barrow Island, November 1985.

Sinclair, J. (1987) An Analysis of Wilderness Policies and Legislation and Preparation for Commonwealth Action. Unpublished report for the Department of Arts, Heritage and the Environment, Canberra.

Sinclair, J. (1986) 'Fraser Island' in Dutton, G. (ed) *The Book of Australian Islands.* Macmillan, Melbourne.

Sinclair, J. (ed) (1971-89) MOONBI: The newsletter of the Fraser Island Defenders Organisation, 1-73.

Skinner, J. E. (May 1974) 'The search for the *Sea Belle* castaways on Fraser Island'. *Queensland Heritage*, Brisbane.

Specht, R. L. (1977) 'Australian heathlands'. *Ecosystems of the World*, 9b, Analytical Studies, Elsevier, Amsterdam.

Specht, R. L., Row, E. M. and Boughton, W. (1974) 'Conservation of major plant communities in Australia and Papua New Guinea'. *Aust. J. Bot.* suppl. series No. 7.

Stanley, T. D. and Ross, E. M. (1984) *Flora of South East Queensland.* Queensland Herbarium, Queensland Department of Primary Industry.

Stanton, J. P. and the Cooloola Committee (1976) *The Conservation of Cooloola.* Queensland Conservation Council.

Stanton, J. P. (1975) A Report on Fraser Island: Natural History, Land Use, Land Classification, and a Framework for its Management. Exhibit No. 9. Fraser Island Environmental Enquiry.

Stephens, A. W., Holmes, A. H. and Jones, M. R. (1988) *Modern Sedimentation and Holocene Shoreline Evolution of the Hervey Bay Coast.* Queensland Department of Mines and Energy.

Tardent, J. L. (1948) Fraser Island. Address to the Royal Geographical Society of Queensland, 7 May 1948.

Thompson, C. H. (1975) 'Coastal areas of southern Queensland some land use conflicts'. *Proc. R. Soc. Qd.* 86:109–20.

Thompson, C. H. (1981) 'Podzol chronosequences on coastal dunes of eastern Australia'. *Nature* 291:59–61.

Thompson, C. H. (1983) 'Development and weathering of large parabolic dune systems along the sub-tropical coast of eastern Australia'. *Z. Geomorph. Suppl.* 45:205–25.

Thompson, C. H. and Hubble, G. D. (1980) 'Sub-tropical podzols (spodosols and related soils) of coastal eastern Australia' in Joseph, K.T. (ed) *Proc. Conf. Class. Manag. Trop. Soils.* Malaysian Soc. Soil. Soc., 203–13.

Thompson, C. H. and Moore, A. W. (1984) 'Studies in landscape dynamics in the Cooloola–Noosa River area. Queensland: 1 Introduction, soil landscapes and research approach' CSIRO Aust. Div. Soils Divl. Rep. No. 73 (in press).

Walker, J., Thompson, C. H., Fergus, I. F. and Tunstall, B. R. (1981) 'Plant succession and soil development in coastal sand dunes of eastern Australia' in West, D. C., Shugart, H. H. and Botkin, D. B. (eds) *Forest Succession: Concepts and Application.* Springer-Verlag, New York, 107–31.

Walker, J. and Thompson, C. H. (1983) 'Possible effects of fire on various phases of vegetation development on sand dunes at Cooloola, Queensland'. *The Second Queensland Fire Research Workshop Proceedings*: 187–203.

Ward, W. T. (1977) 'Sand movement on Fraser Island: a response to changing climates'. University of Queensland, Department of Anthropology, Pap. 8:113–26.

Ward, W. T. and Little, I. P. (1975) 'Times of coastal sand accumulation in south-east Queensland'. *Proc. Ecol. Soc. Aust.* 9:313–17.

Ward, W. T., Little, I. P. and Thompson, C. H. (1979) 'Stratigraphy of two sandrocks at Rainbow Beach, Queensland, Australia, and a note on humate composition'. *Paleogragr., Paleoclimat., Paleoecol.* 26:305–16.

Ward, W. T. (1977) 'Quaternary geology and geomorphology of Fraser Island' in Day, R. H. (ed) *Field Conference: Lady Elliot Island — Fraser Island — Gayndah — Biggenden.* Geological Society of Australia, Queensland Division: 61–4.

Watson, F. J. (1944) *Vocabularies of Four Representative Tribes of South East Queensland.* Royal Geographical Society of Queensland.

Whitehouse, E. W. (1967) 'Wallum country'. *Queensland Naturalist* 18 (3–4):64–72.

Whitehouse, F. W. (1968) 'Fraser Island: geology and geomorphology'. *Queensland Naturalist* 19 (1–3):3–9.

Williams, F. R. (1982) *Written in Sand: History of Fraser Island.* Jacaranda Press, Brisbane.

ENDNOTES

Page 12: The quotation from Judith Wright is from 'The Individual in a New Environmental Age' in *Because I Was Invited* (Oxford University Press, 1975). It is published by permission of the author.

THE GREAT SANDY REGION

Page 27: 'At Coololah' by Judith Wright is from *Collected Poems 1942–70* © Judith Wright, 1971. The extract is reproduced by permission of Collins/Angus & Robertson Publishers.

THE LOST GENERATIONS

Page 47: Dr Norman Tindale's comment is from *Aboriginal Tribes of Australia* (Berkeley, 1974). Archibald Meston's evaluation of the number of Aborigines is from his *Report on Fraser Island*, submitted to the Queensland Legislative Assembly and published by the Government Printer (Brisbane, 1905).

Pages 50 and 52: Rollo Petrie's memories are from personal communication with the author.

Page 56: The *Moreton Bay Courier* report was published on 18 September 1852. It was one of many reports of the conflict between Aborigines and newcomers in 1851–52.

Page 61: The Reverend Fuller published an account of the Aboriginal mission on Fraser Island in the *Brisbane Courier*, 3 October 1872.

Page 62: Archibald Meston's ambitions are from his *Report on the Aboriginal Station Recently Formed on Fraser's Island*, March 1897. For an account of the interaction between Europeans and Aborigines in the region (including the history of the mission settlements), see Raymond Evans and Jan Walker, 'These Strangers, Where Are They Going? Aboriginal–European Relations in the Fraser Island and Wide Bay Region 1770–1905' in *Fraser Island* (Occasional Papers in Anthropology, 8), Anthropology Museum, University of Queensland, 1977.

Page 64: Rollo Petrie's memories are from personal communication with the author.

EXPLORERS AND SETTLERS

Page 74: Cook's impressions are recorded in his *Journal*, edited by W. J. Wharton (London, 1893).

Page 76: Flinders' comments are from *A Voyage to Terra Australis* (London, 1814).

Pages 77 and 81: Eliza Fraser's comments and her somewhat embellished account of her ordeal on Fraser Island are to be found in *The Shipwreck of the Stirling Castle* (London, 1838).

Page 86: Walter Petrie's comments on Fraser Island's timber are from his *Report* to the Queensland Forestry Department.

CLOTHING THE SAND

Page 129: Patrick White's description is from *A Fringe of Leaves* (London, 1976).

Page 138: The article by Dr L. J. Webb and W. T. Williams was published in *Hemisphere*, 1972.

A LAND OF LAKES

Page 192: Kathleen McArthur's description of the Noosa River is from *A Living River: the Noosa* (Caloundra, 1974) published by Kathleen McArthur for the Wildlife Preservation Society of Queensland Inc. Caloundra Branch. It is published by permission of the author.

FISH, FOWL AND OTHER FAUNA

Page 198: Rollo Petrie's memories are from personal communication with the author.

FIGHTING TO THE FUTURE

Pages 238 and 244: Judith Wright's comments are from her submission to the Fraser Island Environmental Inquiry, published in the Transcripts of the Inquiry. They are published here by permission of the author.

ACKNOWLEDGEMENTS

The author wishes to acknowledge the cooperation and help of many people and organisations who assisted in the preparation of this book.

The assistance, comments and corrections of editor, Sheena Coupe, were particularly appreciated, as was the encouragement of Kevin Weldon, one of Australia's most enterprising publishers, in deciding to proceed with this project.

I value also the inspiration and personal encouragement of many great Australian writers who have written eloquently on Fraser Island and Cooloola. These include Patrick White and Judith Wright. The contagious enthusiasm of people such as Rollo Petrie has been equally as inspiring. His seventy-seven years intimate association with Fraser Island have been a model of persistence.

I have appreciated the ready cooperation of a number of the most eminent scientists in their field who have provided advice and information over two decades, thus helping me to reach a better understanding of the complex environment of the Great Sandy Region. I have aknowledged the assistance of many of them in the World Heritage nomination for the region. In addition, Dr A. G. Harrold, of Noosa, was particularly helpful in reviewing Chapter 5 on vegetation, where his expertise is far greater than mine. Dr P. K. Lauer, of the Anthropological Museum, University of Queensland, provided photographic material and a much greater appreciation of the region's Aboriginal cultural heritage.

I have had enormous support from every sector of the voluntary nature conservation movement in Australia in general and Queensland in particular. The support of the Fraser Island Defenders Organisation through two decades has enabled me to develop a much fuller understanding of a complexity of issues which have greatly enriched my life.

John Sinclair
Gladesville, 1990

PICTURE CREDITS

Index

Entries in italics indicate photograph captions.

Aborigines, traditional society 45–54
Acacia sp. 152, *152*
acid frogs 188, 204
Agathis robusta 146
ah-wong 45, 67
Aldridge, Henry 82
amphibia 204–6
Angiopteris evecta see king fern
Angophora costata see smooth-barked apple
angular pigface *129*, *134*, 140
ants 209, *209*, *211*, 212
Aramac (ship) 93
Araucaria cunninghamiana see hoop pine
Archontophoenix cunninghamiana see piccabeen palm
Argyrodendron trifoliolatum 164
Asplenium australasicum see crowsnest fern
Australian Conservation Foundation 228, 230, 246

Backhousia myrtifolia see carrol
Balarrgan 61, 62, 90
bandicoot 198
Banksia aemula 34
Banksia integrifolia 142
Banksia oblongifolia 158
Banksia robur see swamp banksia
Banksia serrata 34, *34*
Banksia spinulosa 36, 152, 164
bar-tailed godwit 204
Barnwall, Sir Reginald 227
barrage lakes 180–3
Basin Lake *169*
bass, Australian 192
bats 198
beach oak 142, *145*
beach primrose *135*, 140
beach spinifex *117*, *129*, 140, 142, *142*
bees, native 51, *52*
Bellert, Hans 94
berms 117
Big Woody Island 51, 68, 95, 200
birds 200–4
Blackall Ranges 45
blackbutt 142, 152, 162
Blechnum fern 50
bloodwood 142, 152
blowouts 120
blue-faced honeyeater *202*
Bogimbah 62, 64, 65, 84, *88*
Bogimbah Creek 172
bolly gum 146
boneseed weed 242
Boomerang Lakes 172
Boon Boon Creek 68, 98
Boonlye Point 34
Boonooroo 20, 34
bora rings 68–70
Boreen Point *41*, *157*, 195, *229*
Boronia keysii 36, 164
Boronia rivularis 36, *134*, 164
Boyungan Rocks Bypass *243*
Bracefell, David 54–6, 78, 81
brahminy kite *197*

Breaksea Spit 24, 90, *91*, 93, 95, *109*
Bribie Island 78, 81
Brown, Robert 76
brumbies 200, 242
brush bronze pigeon 202
brushbox 146, 152, 162
brushbox orchid 146
Bubbler spring *170*, 175
Bufo marinus see cane toad
bumpy ash 146
bunders see convicts, escaped
bushwalking 38
Butchalla Association 70
Butchalla people 47

cabbage palm *see* fan palm
Caboonya *46*
Caladenia carnea see pinkies
Calamoecia tasmanica 209
Callitris columellaris see cypress pine
Calyptorhynchus lathami see glossy black cockatoo
cane toad 206, *206*
canoe trees 68
Carland Creek 84
carpet python *206*
Carpobrotus glaucescens see angular pigface
carrol 146, 152, 164
Casuarina equisetifolia see beach oak
Casuarina glauca see swamp she-oak
Casuarina torulosa see forest oak
Cathedrals *102*, 103, *104*
Caustis blakei see foxtail fern
Central Station *50*, 52, *60*, *148*, *150*, *164*, 227
chainfruit *134*
Chang Chow (ship) 93
Charadrius mongolus see Mongolian sand-plover
Charadrius ruficapillus see red-capped dotterel
Cherbourg 62, 63
Cherry Venture (ship) *93*, 94
Chironomid 209
Christmas orchids *227*
Cinnamomum baileyanum 164
Coaldrake, J. E. 36
cockroach 212
coffee rock 112, *112*, 188
Collembola 212
coloured sand *26*, *40*, *97*, *102*, 103–6, *104*, *124*, *247*
Como Scarp 188
conservation 219–48
convicts, escaped 54–6
Cook, Captain James 20, 47, 74, *75*, 76
Cooloola Committee 219, 222
Cooloola National Park 27, 89, 146, 224, *224*
Cooloola propator 212
Cooloola sand patch 120
Coongul Creek 172
copepod 209
crabapple 146
crabs *214*, 217, *217*, *232*
crested pigeon *203*
crowsnest fern 146
Curtis, John *80*
cypress pine 142, 157, 162

Davis, James 54, 56, 81
Davison, Frank Dalby 180
Dendrobium aemulum see brushbox orchid
Dicksonia youngiae 164
die-back disease 162
Dilli 240
Dillingham 227, 232
Dillingham-Murphyores 228–9, 232
dingo *198*, 200, *201*, 242
Diptera *see* Chironomid
Dipuying 86
Double Island Point 27, 74, 78, 98, 100, 127
Double Island Point lighthouse 21, 94–5
Dream Island 34
Drosera lovellae 164
Drosera sp. *see* rosette sundews
dugong 28, *197*, 212
Dulingbara people 47
Dutch navigators 68, *68*

earthworms 209, *211*, 212
eastern curlew 204, *205*
echidna 198
Edwardson, William 76
eel grass 158, 195
Elanda Plains 224
Elanda Point 82, *194*, 195, *219*
Eli Creek 152, 172, 236, *246*
Eliza Fraser trail 244
elkhorn 146, *236*
Elmer, Gordon 90
emu 198, 200
Emydura kreftii see Kreft's river turtle
Eriostemon australis see pink wax flower
Eucalyptus intermedia see bloodwood
Eucalyptus microcorys see tallowwood
Eucalyptus pilularis see blackbutt
Eucalyptus signata see scribbly gum
Eucalyptus tessellaris see Moreton Bay ash
Eurong 24, 82, 90, 227, 228, 240
Euroschinus falcatus see ribbonwood
Everglades *192*
everlasting daisies *132*, *144*

Falco peregrinus see peregrine falcon
fan palm 152
fauna 197–217
fawn-footed melomys 198, *199*
feldspars 102, 132, 136
feral animals 200, 240, 242
ferries 240–2
Ficus watkinsiana see strangler fig
FIDO *see* Fraser Island Defenders Organisation
fish 188, 209
Fisheries Habitat Reserves 34, 242
fishing, commercial 34, 217
fishing, sport 36–8, *38*, *39*, 217, *217*, *233*, *241*, *249*
Flagellaria indica see Indian lawyer vine
Flinders, Matthew 47, 61, 74–6, *74*
Flindersia schottiana see bumpy ash
forest oak 152
forestry *see* timber industry
Forestry Department, Queensland 162, 224, 227, 238, 240
Foulmouth Creek 86
foxtail fern 142

Fraser, Eliza 56, 76–81, 77, *80*
Fraser, Captain James 56, 76–81, *79*
Fraser Island Defenders Organisation 219,
 227–30, 232, 236, 246, *246*
Fraser Island Recreation Board 232
Fraser Island Recreation Management Plan
 236
frogs 204
fruit bat, grey-headed 198
Fuller, Reverend William 61

Gahnia sieberiana see swordgrass
Garrys Camp 70, 244
geebung 152
geology 98–100
Geoscapheus primulatus see cockroach
glider, yellow-bellied 197
glossy black cockatoo 202
Gmelina leichhardtii 164
goannas *207*
goats 200
goatsfoot convolvulus 140, *141*
Graham, John 54, 78
grass owl 202
Great Barrier Reef 24, 27, 31, 40, *213*, 246
Great Sandy National Park 24, 146, 158,
 236, *237*
Great Sandy Strait 20, 31, 34, 76, 82, 202,
 204, 212, 242
Grevillea hilliana 164
ground parrot 36, 202
gunyah trees 68
Gympie 81, 82, 222

Hakea gibbosa 137
Hammerstone sandblow *121*
Happy Valley 24, 90, 227, 228, 240
Harrold, Dr Arthur 219, 222
Harry's Hut 192
heathland 157
Helichrysum bracteatum see everlasting daisies
Hervey, John Augustus 20
Hervey Bay 20, 28, *28*, *29*, 31, *31*, 40, 74,
 82, 212
Hervey Bay (town) 20, *21*, 36, *202*, 236
Hibbertia 52
Hidden Lake 186
High Court of Australia 228, 230
Hook Point *15*, *73*, 95, 152, *156*, *158*, *214*,
 215, 240
hoop pine 152, *153*, 162, 164, *234*
horsetail oak *see* beach oak
humate *see* coffee rock
Huxley, Bill and Mavis 219
hydrology 170–83
hyphae 136

ilmenite 98, *103*
Indian Head 70, *75*, 82, 98, 100, *100*, 117,
 127, *241*
Indian lawyer vine 146
Inskip Point 90, 95, 127, 222, 232, 240
invertebrates 209
Ipomea pes-caprae see goatsfoot convolvulus

jellyfish *214*, *215*

Kabi-Kabi people 47, 54, *55*
kauri pine 28, 34, *58*, 146, 162, 164
Kgari trail 244
Kin Kin Creek 152, 158, 172
Kinaba Information Centre *225*, 244
king fern *150*, 164
Kirrar sandblow *125*
Knifeblade sandblow *123*
koala 198
Korainga 240
Kreft's river turtle *208*

Laguna Bay 127, 192
Lake Benaroon 186
Lake Birrabeen 70, 175, *176*, 179, 183, 236
Lake Boomanjin *166*, 172, *174*, *175*, 183,
 186, 209, 236, *237*, *238*
Lake Bowaraddy 152, 162
Lake Como 20, 195
Lake Cooloola 20, 195
Lake Coomboo 188, *208*
Lake Cooriobah 20, 192, 195
Lake Cootharaba 20, *41*, 78, 82, *83*, 158,
 169, 172, 192, *192*, 195, *195*, *219*,
 224, *229*
Lake Doonella 192, 195
Lake Freshwater 180
Lake Jennings 175
Lake McKenzie *25*, *178*, 179, *179*, *182*, 183,
 186, 236
Lake Poona 183, *185*
Lake Tewantin 192
Lake Wabby *15*, *43*, *45*, 120, *121*, 157, 158,
 180, 186, 209, 236
Lake Wanhar 244
Lake Weyba 61, 195
lakes, barrage *see* barrage lakes
lakes, perched *see* perched lakes
lakes, river *see* river lakes
lakes, window *see* window lakes
Lakes of Figtree 188
Lands Department, Queensland 227, 228,
 238
Lauer, Dr Peter 65
Lawrence, D. H. 180
Leptospermum sp. *36*, 152, *152*, 157
lichen *150*, *155*, *156*
lighthouses 94–5
lillypilly, small-leaved *150*
Limosa lapponica see bar-tailed godwit
Litoria peronii 206
Litsea leefeana see bolly gum
Livistona australis see fan palm
loggerhead sea turtle 212
logging *see* timber industry
Lophostemon confertus see brushbox

Maaroom 20, 242
McArthur, Kathleen 192
McKechnie, Peter 236
McKenzie, H. 86
McKenzie's jetty *89*, 90
Macquaria novemaculeata see bass, Australian
macrozamia *21*, 140, 152
Maheno (ship) *92*, 93–4
mammals 197–200
management principles 246–7

mangrove *30*, *33*, 34, 52, *73*, 158, *158*, *159*,
 161, 164, 217, *217*
Marloo (ship) 93
Marsdenia glandulifera 164
Mary Ann (locomotive) 84
Mary River 31, 34, 40, 56, 64, *84*, 86, 89
Maryborough 62, 81, 82, 86, 89, 236
Megaptera novaeangliae 31
melaleuca *41*, *43*, *110*, *129*, 142, *143*, 157,
 158, 162, 169, *169*, 175 *175*, *192*, *234*
Melaleuca quinquenervia see melaleuca
Melicope octandra 164
Melomys cervinipes see fawn-footed melomys
Mendonca, Christado de 73
Meston, Archibald 47, 61, 180
Meston, Harold 61–2, 64
middens, Aboriginal 61, 65, *65*, *67*, 68, *69*,
 217
Middle Rocks *16*, *51*
Mill Point *49*, *83*
minerals 90, 98, 103, 132, 136, 140, 230
missions, Aboriginal 61–4
Mon Repos 28, 212
Mongolian sand-plover 204
Moon Boon Islands 34
Moon Point 127
Moonaboola River 81
Moreton Bay 54, 76, 81
Moreton Bay ash 142
Mount Bilewilam 192
Mudlo Rocks 70, 110
Murphyores 227, 232
musk duck 188

National Parks and Wildlife Service,
 Queensland 224, 236, 238
Nauruan settlement 227
Neophema pulcella see turquoise parrot
Newman, Kevin 40
Ngulungbara people 47
Ninox plumiferus see powerful owl
Nolan, Sidney 79
Noosa Heads 18, 20, 27, 36, 57, 61, 78
Noosa Parks Association *219*, 222
Noosa River *20*, 27, 36, 45, *57*, 152, 157,
 158, 172, 188–92, *189*, *191*, 195, *195*,
 209, 224, *225*
North White Cliffs 56, 61, 62, 82, 84, 86,
 236
Nugget (Aborigine) 50–1, *63*, 198
Numenius madagascariensis see eastern curlew
nutrients, plant 138–40, 179

Ocean Lake 158, 186, *219*
oceanic sands 103, 106, 110
Ocyphaps lophotes see crested pigeon
Oenothera drummondii see beach primrose
oil exploration 90
Oodgeroo Noonuccal 169
Orchid beach *217*, 222
Orchid Beach (town) 24, 90, 227, 228, 240
Ostreidae sp. 68, 74
Otter, Lieutenant 78
Owens, 'Banjo' Henry 64

Panama (ship) 90
pandanus 52, *53*, 142, *142*
paperbark *see* melaleuca

Patersonia sericea see pink iris
peat 172
pelican 195, *200*
perched lakes *169*, 172, 180–3, 186
peregrine falcon 202
Peron's tree frog 206
Petaurus australis see glider, yellow-bellied
Petrie, Andrew 56, 81, 82
Petrie, Rollo 50–1, 52, 64, 198
Petrie, Tom 58
Petrie, Walter 86
Pettigrew and Sim 84
Pezoporus wallicus see ground parrot
Phaps elegans see brush bronze pigeon
Phebalium billardieri 164
Phebalium woombye 164
piccabeen palm 146, *150*
Piggott, 'Yankee Jack' 58, 61
pink iris *135*
pink pimelia *132*
pink wax flower *135*
pinkies *133*
Planchonella australis 164
platypus 198
Platypus Bay 31, 212
Plebidonax deltoides 67, 68
plumed frogmouth 202
Podargus ocellatus plumiferus see plumed
    frogmouth
podzols 124, 136–8, 164, 172, 179, 209
Poona 20
Portuguese explorers 73
Poverty Point 84
powerful owl 202
Pteroporus poliocephalus see fruit bat, grey-
    headed
Pyrazus ebeninus 68

QTM *see* Queensland Titanium Mines
quandong *164*
Queensland Titanium Mines 228

rabbits 200
Rainbow beach 74, 103, *106*, *247*
Rainbow Beach (town) 20, 36, 222, 240,
    242
Rainbow Gorge *170*
rainbow lorikeet *202*
rainforest 146, *147*, *148*, *149*, 152, 164, *234*,
    236
Ramsay, John 82
Ramsays Scrub 82, 152
Red Lagoon 209
red-capped dotterel *204*
Register of the National Estate 230, 232
reptiles 204–6
rhyolite 98–9, *99*
ribbonwood 146
Ricinocarpos pinifolius see wedding bush
river lakes 195
rodents, native 198
Rooney Point 61, 127, 217
rosette sundews *136*
Russell, Henry Stuart 81
rutile 90, 98, 103, *103*

sand 15–18, 97–127
sand dunes 97, 106–10, 112, 117–20, 138,
    140, 142, 170
sand monitors *see* goannas
sand swimmers 209
sandblows *16*, *19*, *97*, *110*, *116*, 120–4, 140,
    157, *230*
    see also Hammerstone sandblow; Kirrar
    sandblow; Knifeblade sandblow
sandmining 90, 103, 222, 224, 227–30, 232,
    236, 240
Sandy Cape 20, 21, 24, 61, 70, 74, 90, 117,
    212
Sandy Cape lighthouse 21, 24, 91, *91*, 93,
    94, 95, *95*, 158
satinay *42*, *50*, 52, *58*, 86–7, *86*, 146, 162,
    163, 164
scented fan flower 140
Schizomeria ovata see crabapple
sclerophyll forest 152
screwpine *see* pandanus
scribbly gum 142, 152, 164
scrub turkey 198
Seabelle (ship) 58
seagrass 158, 217
Seary, Pat 94
Searys Creek 172
Searys Scrub 84
sedge *166*
shipwrecks 58, 76–81, 90–4
Sinclair, John 228
skinks 206
smooth-barked apple 142, 152
snakes 206
southern emu wren 200
Sowerbaea juncea see vanilla lily
Spinifex sericeus see beach spinifex
springtails *see* Collembola
staghorn 146
Stanton, J. P. 232
Stewart Island 34
Stipiturus malachurus see southern emu wren
Stirling Castle (ship) 56, 76, *80*, 81
Stradbroke Island 169
strangler fig 146, *154*, 164
succession, plant 140–6
Supreme Court, Queensland 222, 228, 232
swamp banksia 157, *157*, 162
swamp box 152, 162
swamp fern *166*
swamp she-oak 158
swamp wallaby 198
swordgrass 157
Syncarpia hillii see satinay

tallowwood 152, 162
Tecomanthe hillii 164
Teewah 20
Teewah beach 74, 78, *93*, 94, 127, *170*, 175
termites 212
Tewah Creek 172, 188, 192
Tewantin 70
Tiaro 56
timber industry 58–61, *58*, 82–9, *83*, *84*, *85*,
    88, *89*, 162–3, 224–7, 232
Tin Can Bay 20, 27, 31, 34, 40, 68, 70, 98,
    172, 192, 202

Tin Can Bay (town) 34
Tindale, Dr Norman 47
Tinnanbar 20
tourism 24, 36–8, 90, 232, 240
Trichoglossus haemotodus see rainbow lorikeet
turquoise parrot 202
turtle, freshwater 188, *188*
turtle, loggerhead 28, *29*
Tyto longimembris see grass owl

Ungowa 21, 24
Urang Creek *63*
Urangan 89
Utricularia 136

vanilla lily *135*
vegetation 129–66
vine forest *see* rainforest
Voulden, Harry 81

Waddy Point 16, 70, 77, 98, *118*, 127, 212,
    233
waders 202–4
Waiwera (ship) 93
Walameboulha Lagoon *166*
Walker, Frederick 58
Walker, Kath 169
Wallabia bicolor see swamp wallaby
wallum 34–6, *34*
Wanggoolba Creek *24*, *148*, *150*, 172, 227,
    236, 242
Ward, Bill 73
water, black *170*, 175, *175*, 179
water, white 175, 179
water rat, Australian 198
water rat, false 197
Wathumba Creek 31, *45*, 115, 152, 157,
    158, *158*, *159*, *161*, 172, *173*, *214*,
    217, 228, 231
Watson, F. J. 47
Webb, Dr L. J. 138, 146
wedding bush *134*
whale, humpback 31, *31*, 212, *212*, *213*
White, Patrick 129
white beech 162
Whitlam, Gough 228
Wide Bay 74, 90, 127, 152
wilderness values 238–46
wildflowers 132, *132*, 157, *224*
Williams, W. T. 138
window lakes 180
Womalah landscape 36, 198, 224
Woody Island 31, 34
Woralie Creek 172
World Heritage significance 40–3, 164, 246
Wright, Judith 12, 27, 238, 240, 244
Wyvill, Les 228

xanthorrhoea 52, *52*
Xanthostemon oppositifolius 164
Xeromys myoides see water rat, false

Yankee Jack Lake 183
Yankee Jack's Creek 82, 172

Z Force 90
zircon 90, 98, 103